Your LIFE Your LEGACY

A Legal Handbook

Darra Lynn Rayndon, Esq.

DISCLAIMER

This book has been prepared for informational purposes only, and nothing in it may be considered legal advice. Readers should not act upon information contained herein without seeking professional legal and tax advice.

Any communication regarding this book does not create an attorney-client relationship with the authors or their firms, and therefore, no attorney-client privilege is attached by communication about the book and its contents.

In accordance with the Internal Revenue Service Circular 230, rules of practice before the IRS, if this book contains any type of tax information, please be advised that, based on current IRS rules and standards, the information contained herein is not tax advice and is not intended to be used, nor can it be used, for the avoidance of any tax penalty that the IRS may assess related to any matter.

Published by Premier Graphics Publishing

ISBN#978-0-983299-7-6-9

THE AUTHORS

 Author, Attorney **Darra Lynn Rayndon**, of Rayndon Law Group PLC, Scottsdale, Arizona, has over three decades of law practice experience. Certified as a Tax Specialist by the Arizona Bar, Ms. Rayndon received her J.D. degree from the University of Wisconsin Law School and her LL.M. (Tax) degree from Georgetown University Law Center. Darra founded Rayndon Law Group PLC, a Martindale-Hubbell A-V rated firm, more than 25 years ago. Ms. Rayndon's work includes tax planning, business entity formation and representation, estate and wealth succession planning, estate and trust administration and fiduciary services, asset protection, real estate, and private securities offerings. She is also an Arizona Licensed Fiduciary. She presently is a member of the Women Presidents' Organization, Central Arizona Estate Planning Council, local tax and financial groups, and the Board of Trustees for Desert Botanical Garden, and she is current chair of its Planned Giving Committee. A frequent lecturer, Ms. Rayndon is regularly invited to speak at seminars on estate planning and taxation, domestic and off-shore asset protection and corporate issues. Her sequel to this book is slated for publication in 2014. Ms. Rayndon's important messages on life, financial, and estate planning can be heard regularly on her radio show, "Darra Speaks...Money and the Law," at DoublewideNetwork.com.

Contributing author, Attorney **David P. Arrow**, a native Chicagoan, has practiced law for over 30 years, focusing his practice on family, juvenile, probate, trust and estate matters. He also served for many years as a family mediator. He joined Rayndon Law Group PLC after retiring from the Maricopa County Superior Court in 2007. His work presently concentrates on trust administration, conservatorships and guardianships, estate planning, commercial transactions, marital agreements and Qualified Domestic Relations Orders (QDROs). Mr. Arrow earned his undergraduate degree at the University of Illinois, his JD degree at IIT-Chicago Kent College of Law, his Master's degree from the University of New Mexico and his PhD (ABD) from Arizona State University. He taught for many years at Arizona State University and Scottsdale Community College. He has been admitted to practice in Illinois, New Mexico, Arizona and the United State Supreme Court. He has served as Chairman of the State Foster Care Review Board and the Casey Family Program and has served on numerous court-improvement and child welfare boards, task forces and commissions, and bar association committees.

Contributing author, Attorney **Michelle Margolies Tran**, admitted to practice before the Arizona Supreme Court, the United States Tax Court, and the United States District Court in Arizona, received her law degree from the Arizona State University College of Law and her Masters of Laws (LL.M.) in taxation from the University of Florida College of Law. Ms. Tran practices law with Rayndon Law Group PLC and focuses in the areas of estate and tax planning for individuals, families, and businesses. She also provides legal services in business formation and transfers, trust administration, and probate.

Ms. Tran received her undergraduate degree from the University of California, San Diego.

 Contributing author, Attorney **Allyson Joy Teply**, joined Rayndon Law Group PLC in 2005 after receiving her law degree from Arizona State University College of Law. She was a William H. Pedrick Scholar and concentrated her studies in estate planning and taxation. She received her Bachelor of Science degree in Psychology from the University of Arizona. Ms. Teply's work focuses in the areas of estate, tax, and business planning. As well as estate and trust administration, probate, fiduciary services, and asset protection. Ms. Teply is an Arizona native, actively involved in her community.

 Contributing author, Attorney **Ely W. Sluder**, received his law degree from the Arizona State University College of Law in 2003 where he focused his studies on business, internet law, real estate and intellectual property. Prior to attending law school, Mr. Sluder received his Bachelor of Science degree in Human Communication with an emphasis on rhetoric and conflict resolution from Arizona State University in 2000. Mr. Sluder is also a veteran, having served as a Combat Medic in the U.S. Army from 1992-1995. After receiving his law degree, Mr. Sluder spent time as General Counsel for an internet company and as General Manager/General Counsel for a licensed real estate brokerage firm before joining Rayndon Law Group PLC. Mr. Sluder currently focuses his practice on business, contract, real estate and intellectual property law. He typically handles client issues such as mergers and acquisitions, asset sales and purchases, business entity formations, private offerings, commercial leases and general contract drafting and review. He bills himself as

a "virtual in-house counsel," able to help solve a very wide range of problems for businesses and their owners.

Contributing author, Attorney **Marsha Goodman**, a sole practitioner in Phoenix, Arizona, is a summa cum laude graduate of St. Lawrence University in Canton, New York and the Vanderbilt University School of Law in Nashville, Tennessee. Her practice includes traditional elder law services, such as Guardianships and Conservatorships, Powers of Attorney and other Advance Directives, and assisting clients file claims and resolve disputes regarding Medicaid, Medicare, Veterans' Benefits, Social Security and other public benefits. In addition, her staff includes human services professionals who work with Ms. Goodman and clients' families to combine asset protection, public benefits qualification, insurance assistance, nursing home advocacy and crisis intervention into a comprehensive package called a Life Care Plan. Ms. Goodman has been admitted to practice in both Michigan and Arizona. She is member of the National Academy of Elder Law Attorneys and serves on the Board of Directors of the Life Care Planning Law Firms Association. Ms. Goodman is a member of the Maricopa County and Arizona State Bar Associations. She has been appointed to the Military Legal Assistance Committee, and the Executive Council of the Probate and Trust Committee, both part of the Arizona Bar Association. Ms. Goodman provides pro bono services through the Maricopa County Bar Association Probate Legal Assistance Project. She has attended the Straus Institute for Dispute Resolution at Pepperdine University School of Law and serves as a volunteer mediator for the Arizona Attorney General's Office.

FOREWORD

I was encouraged to write this book by my spouse David and by members of the Phoenix Chapter of the Women Presidents' Organization ("WPO"). I stalled for a long time, hesitant to put in the effort when so much of my time was and is being spent practicing law, managing a law office, and accumulating the collection of knowledge and client stories which are found in these pages. But, once I got started, I realized that writing this book was a pretty easy task because what I have written are the various messages I have delivered to more than 7,000 clients for more than 25 years.

My initial working title of the book was "You Don't Know What You Don't Know (And You Don't Know When You Don't Know It!)" which I thought was a good starting title because it set up the premise for the book: an informed person will make better decisions about planning and about use of the right planning tools. My work over the years and now with this book has been about helping people achieve their goals in providing for themselves and their families, protecting what they've earned, securing the future, and donating to charities, through legal documents. I shared this title with several people who were accepting of it but not enthusiastic. Truly I thought it was a great title. But then a wise person who has written several books himself suggested that a better title would be "Know What You Don't Know," perhaps a kinder, gentler message. That phrase took me to another title, "Knowing," which is easy, conveys the vision, and wraps up all of the messages into one word. Then I realized that while knowing or knowledge is something you, the reader, need to have in order to properly plan your estate and your business, such planning is about a much bigger picture including yourself, your family, your employees, your causes, etc. My friend Sharon suggested the more expansive title and it stuck. The phrase, "You Don't Know What You Don't Know," became a submessage to the main goal of giving readers legal information for making important and strategic decisions in your lives and for your legacy.

Many people have been helpful to me: my spouse David, and all my fellow WPO members, with special mention of Sharon, Karie, Tami, and Kim Marie; Sue, who explained the ease of publishing; my law partners for their contributions and edits; Dave and Sandy for their nice comments; Marsha who wanted to be a part of it; Tim for his ideas; Mary, Rena, Pamela, Francine and AnneMarie of the 10% Club for their encouragement and wonderful suggestions; Donna who thoughtfully read and edited; and many others. Thank you all very much!

Darra Rayndon
July 2013

Contact us at:
Rayndon Law Group PLC
5001 N. Granite Reef Road
Scottsdale, Arizona 85250

Phone: 480-994-5600
Email: askdarra@gmail.com
www.rayndon.com

A LEGAL HANDBOOK
TABLE OF CONTENTS

INTRODUCTION

YOU DON'T KNOW WHAT YOU DON'T KNOW (AND YOU DON'T KNOW WHEN YOU DON'T KNOW IT!)

1

This book is about estate planning, tax planning, asset protection and similar topics. Its purposes are to make sense of the myriad of rules and planning tools out there, which confound the layperson on a frequent, if not daily, basis; to dispel myths and other pieces of misinformation; and to give you the reader some great ideas for setting up your own personal, tax and business planning. Fully read the book or use it as a handbook, a reference guide, or a way to confirm information you already have. Many topics overlap so you may read similar information in various spots in the book. The idea is to cover as many issues as possible under each main topic in order to give the reader a better understanding of how all of the legal and tax pieces fit together.

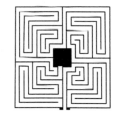

The sentiment expressed by the title of this chapter is very true. It's one of those things about humans that we have not yet fully developed: you do not know those things which you do not know. A companion phrase to the title may be, "you can't believe everything you hear," but what actually happens is that people go to seminars, or read a book on a subject, surf the internet or hear a blurb on a news report, and when they are remembering what they thought they heard or read, it's wrong! The speaker or writer may have been absolutely correct, or may have stated the main rule without the one hundred and one exceptions, and then the lay listener, in taking in new information or processing the new information with old information or in remembering that he had heard that factoid before, will confuse the information, turn it upside down on its head, or forget the exceptions, which often can be more important than the rule. The end result is misinformation which is then spread about when he tells his neighbor, brother-in-law, co-worker, etc. Without proper clarification and without consulting about his own personal situation, the lay listener will go blithely forth in ignorance, thinking he has knowledge, when in fact, he does not know that he does not know what it is that he thinks he knows.

The other piece of the title is also an accurate statement. If you don't know about a rule or situation, there is no little bell or buzzer or siren which goes off in your brain that warns, "There's something out there that you don't know on this subject." There are plenty of things out there that we know that we have no knowledge of, and we may not even know the unknown thing, idea or concept exists. So we know that we don't know about it. But, in dealing with your estate plan, for example, or a business buy-out, you will not be aware of all the myriad rules to come into play. What the heck is the Rule Against Perpetuities anyway?

It is important at this point, in the beginning, to define "lay listener" (or reader or person in general). There are plenty of very smart, bright, educated people who are just as "lay" on these subjects as the person who tunes out everything. The examples are numerous: the educator and business coach who thinks his living trust provides asset protection for him; or the personal injury lawyer who believes that because she does not have a taxable estate, her Will automatically does not have to go through probate; or the retired school teacher who won't do a Will because that will mean "probate," seemingly a dastardly word; or the nurse who won't sign a Living Will because he does not want his family to have to be involved in his death decisions (hint: it's the other way around). Well, that's enough examples for the moment. As you can probably guess, each of these beliefs or understandings is incorrect. In this book, we will set the record straight on those and other tidbits of misinformation and provide some simple straightforward pieces of advice on how to utilize the tools of estate planning, tax planning, and asset protection strategies to get where you need to be. It is designed to give you the information you need to make constructive suggestions and ask knowledgeable questions when working with your advisors. By the way, as an aside, probate can be a good thing. Read on.

The materials you will find herein (that's a lawyer word!) are based on the United States federal tax system and a selection of state laws. As each country has its own sets of laws stemming from its developmental history, non-U.S. readers or U.S. readers with foreign holdings are encouraged to consult with trained professionals in your jurisdiction or in the jurisdictions where you own property or have accounts.

This book is based on the experiences and writings of the primary author, the firm's attorneys, and another colleague, all of whom over the years have worked with clients, spoken at various engagements, and authored white papers. All of the case studies are true, with the names of the parties changed to protect the confidentiality of their stories (as required by our attorney-client relationship). The planning ideas set forth are mainstream and not mere figments of the author's or others' imaginations. Not all of the ideas have been tested either in court or through challenge by the Internal Revenue Service ("IRS"). Frankly, either of those situations are the last thing an attorney wants to see happen to her clients. But, the IRS does not challenge every planning idea, and while a level of caution is always advised, one should not go through life wasting good opportunities because one day the IRS may question a practice or a real creditor or frivolous claimant may file a lawsuit. Planning at least gives you options, whereas no planning leaves you dangling. Ben Franklin may have summarized it best: "By failing to prepare, you are preparing to fail."

This is a good spot in the book to state clearly that no legal advice is offered or provided to you in this writing. Please do not rely solely on what is contained in these pages for your planning, as every person's situation is very different from the next. Each reader is encouraged to consult with her own legal counsel, hopefully one schooled in tax, estate planning, business and asset protection laws. For example, you don't want your endocrinologist doing arthroscopic surgery on that tricky knee. Both are doctors, but their knowledge bases are very different from each other. The situation with attorneys is similar, and it is important that you don't select just any attorney, but rather, that you are able to identify the right attorney for your situation. The information contained in this book is designed to give you the ability to confidently determine whether a particular lawyer is knowledgeable enough to help you.

2 THE BASICS

To get started, let's say firmly that EVERYONE needs an estate plan consisting of documents that accomplish the following (which we will call the "Basics"):

- a primary estate planning document, whether it's a Will or a revocable living trust or similar instrument;

- a general power of attorney, made durable, so that someone else can make financial decisions and take action for you if you get a bump on the head or are otherwise unavailable (think about being out of the country or away from internet service);

- a health care or medical power of attorney, which includes mental health care provisions, so that someone else can make medical decisions for you if you cannot make those decisions for yourself; and

- a living will statement (called a declaration or advanced directive in some states) which defines the medical treatment you wish to have if you are in the dying process, an irreversible coma, or a persistent vegetative state.

- a burial or cremation statement which says what you want and names someone with authority to carry out your wishes, so that all family members do not have to consent to cremation (often required under state law) and to avoid conflicts (you'd be amazed at the possibilities).

You may think that all you have is a cat and a plant, but you actually have more than that or may in death have more than that, so you need to have at least a Will. Your Will is your personal statement concerning whom you wish to administer your affairs at death, and how you want your assets – yes, the cat and the plant, plus that other stuff you don't think about– distributed when you are no longer with us. Even a small, small estate has issues which can be resolved easier with a Will.

If you are married, a "sweetheart" Will is all right to have. That's a Will which leaves everything to your spouse. It will accomplish most of what is needed. A joint Will (one document) with your spouse, however, is a difficult document to administer at the death of one. Two separate Wills make more sense.

Without a doubt, everyone, at a minimum needs a Will. The reasons are numerous and often hard to foresee.

Four Sisters' Story. Three sisters were in a quandary. Their fourth sister, the eldest, had just died at 93 years of age. The deceased, Emily, did not have a Will, at least not that anyone could find. But, she had a bank account of $3,896 in her own name, a $10,000 life insurance policy which named her long-deceased mother as the sole beneficiary, a house with one of the sisters, Anne, named (unbeknownst to Anne) as joint tenant with right of survivorship, household effects, some jewelry with a modicum of dollar value, and a dog. Emily lived simply on her Social Security check and a small pension, both of which stopped at her death. The sisters wanted the lawyer to tell them what to do. The bank would not give any of them the money; the insurance company would not pay the policy proceeds; property taxes were due on the house; there were family issues regarding who got the jewelry; and no one really wanted the dog, who was aged and had bad breath. Oh, yes, and there was concern that the hospital had given their sister the wrong medication which quickened her death. This was like a law school "spot the issues" exam, except that it was real life.

Each separate asset and the rules surrounding its transfer were analyzed to determine the best way to proceed. Clearly many hours of lawyer time were needed for this tiny estate, but as much needed to be done for this estate as is needed for one with more money in the bank account, more insurance, and a significant wrongful death claim. A person needs a Will so he or she can decide what to do with the assets rather than letting the state decide. Emily either just did not think about it or thought she did not need to have a Will. And forget about seeing a lawyer, who as a group are scary and wear gray suits and shout on TV. So, here's how a Will would have helped Emily's family. A Will would have:

- named a personal representative (executor) to serve without bond, who would be in charge of the estate, and be able to address a claim against the hospital;

- determined distribution of the bank account and life insurance policy proceeds;

- determined who got of the jewelry or provided a system for the personal representative to follow; and

- stated who was to take care of the dog and provided funds for his care.

If a probate action (*see* discussion in Chapter 3 about what probate really is) were needed with the Will, it could be, in most states, simple and straightforward, without a large expense.[1] Instead, because Emily died intestate (the legal term meaning "to die without a Will"), no one was named to be the personal representative. The remaining sisters agreed that one of them, Sue, would take the helm and try to accomplish what she could. The sisters had lost a brother many years before, and he had five adult children. Each of them needed to be contacted, although they had never seen nor spoken to Aunt Emily because their father was estranged from his family, but their signatures were needed on documents to enable Sue to have access to the bank account and the insurance policy proceeds. They each ended up receiving a tiny piece of Emily's very small estate, something she probably would not have wanted.

Regarding the life insurance, fortunately the issuing insurance company had an internal rule that if the named beneficiary was deceased, as in this case, the proceeds would be paid to the estate of the insured. Thus, Sue as the personal representative, was able to receive the $10,000 from the insurance policy as part of the estate and to use some of those funds to pay for Emily's funeral, her outstanding bills, estate administration costs, and greatly discounted legal fees. She had to distribute the remaining estate in equal shares to the sisters and the children of the deceased brother, by the laws of intestate succession (meaning who gets assets if someone dies intestate). Each of them, therefore, received cash from

---

1 Each state has its own probate rules. Some are simpler and less costly than others. Probate should generally be started in the deceased's state of residency with an ancillary probate opened in other states where the deceased owned real property.

Emily's estate. Anne got the house In addition and was responsible for the property taxes. Since she had no funds with which to pay the taxes, she had to sell the house in a down market as the only way to deal with her new asset. The jewelry went to those who wanted it, and a friend took the dog, but without any funds for his care.

Let's look for comparison at a well-planned estate which went smoothly.

Dorothy's Story. Dorothy lived a comfortable, simple life as a widow. She had leukemia in remission and enjoyed her neighbors and browsing the local malls. She had three adult sons, who worked and lived in another state. She emphatically did not want to be a burden to her sons and consulted with an estate planning attorney about the best course of action. Because it was possible that she could become incapacitated as her disease progressed, the attorney recommended the use of a revocable living trust as her primary estate planning document, to avoid not only probate but also a conservatorship if she became unable to handle her affairs. She made an effort to understand the process, communicated with her sons, and approved the plan. Her revocable living trust named all three of her sons as successor co-trustees, to act in her place once she could no longer serve as her own trustee. It's not always a good idea to have so many trustees, but she knew it would be meaningful to her sons and that they would all get along well in the process. The attorney helped her transfer her titled property to the trust, in order to avoid the need for a probate. Fortunately, she did not undergo any extended period of disability, so her sons did not need to take over management of her affairs until her death. Because of the careful planning that took place by Dorothy, her sons clearly knew what they needed to do at her demise. The sons had one meeting for 30 minutes In the attorney's office, in which most of the time was spent talking about what a great person their mother was, and two follow-up phone calls. Attorney fees for settling the estate were minimal because Dorothy had engaged the attorney early to get everything set up, and there was no need for any court process. Not all situations can be anticipated, but planning in advance, like Dorothy did, always pays.

For many people, however, the Basics list may need to be expanded somewhat, depending on your circumstances. If you have a child with special needs, a taxable estate, a business which you own, real estate in multiple states, an inheritance with a power of appointment connected to it, or other circumstances, your list of requirements will be longer. These and other planning concepts and methods are discussed in greater detail in subsequent chapters.

Discussion About Trusts

You will see the word <u>trust</u> used a great deal in this book in reference to a type of legal concept or document. There are many types of trusts so at the basic level it's important to know just what a trust is. A proper trust has a creator, the Trustor; a person who holds a property interest for another, the Trustee; and the person with the beneficial interest being held, the Beneficiary. In a trust, there is a special relationship formed among these three parties in which the trustee has a fiduciary duty to the beneficiary to administer the trust according to its governing terms, not to self-deal or be negligent, and generally to protect the property of the trust.

Trusts can have many different features, but they all have a Trustor, a Trustee, and a Beneficiary, of some sort. The trust can be oral or written, revocable or irrevocable, living or testamentary, short-term or very long-term. It can hold all types of property, from houses to stocks and bonds, cash, precious metals, art, jewelry, debt instruments, businesses, insurance, land and more. Throughout the following chapters, in the discussions and stories in this book, trusts will be described and talked about. As you read about the various types of trusts, think of the three players – the Trustor (creator) Trustee (administrator), and the Beneficiary (recipient) – for enhanced understanding of this vital tool of estate planning.

Urban Myths

There are many "urban myths" about estate plans that should be debunked. Misinformation can be very costly, and consequences of poor planning can be even more extreme than the example of the four sisters given above.

Estate planning simply means

• having a Will and possibly a revocable living trust;

• designating your beneficiaries properly in pension plans, Individual Retirement Accounts, life insurance policies, annuities, and pay-on-death (POD) or transfer-on-death (TOD) accounts;

• titling assets to reflect your plan, including the use of beneficiary deeding or deeds with right of survivorship ("WROS") designations such as joint tenancy with right of survivorship or community property with right of survivorship;

• providing a means of payment of debts and estate taxes, if any;

• stating your burial or cremation or other disposition wishes with a designated person to carry out your wishes; and

• having general and health care powers of attorney and living wills.

Here are some of the excuses we hear as to why people don't have estate plans.

"I don't have enough assets."

The parents of a 20-year-old young man seriously injured in a car accident could not make medical and care decisions for their son or have access to his small bank account without getting a costly court order. The point is that most of us have more than we think, and all of us have our bodies for which we may need care decisions one day. In the case of the person in this example, once a person turns 18, he is considered legally an adult, so no one can act for him without either permission in a legal document or a court order.

"I am superstitious: if I sign a Will, I will die."

Rationally, we all know we will each die one day, and the act of signing a Will is probably not going to be the thing that ends your life. You add to your estate plan every time you make a significant purchase, name a beneficiary, take title to your house or car, etc. Be sure it's all done and done correctly. A childless 80-year-old with a nice size estate died leaving no Will because of her superstition. Her estate escheated or was distributed to her state of residency because there were no known beneficiaries. Her favorite charities received nothing.

"Let the kids handle it. After all, I won't be here."

It will cost a lot of your hard-earned money to fix problems caused by poor or non-existent estate planning once you are gone. A gentleman died intestate, without a Will, because he thought his children would simply take his property and split it among themselves. His adult children are now fighting in court over his assets rather than remembering their father fondly.

"I will do it later, or I don't want to think about it right now, or I am too busy, or that's for old people."

Life is fragile. One look at a day's obituaries in your local newspaper shows that death does not occur at any certain age late in life. For example, an unmarried 42-year-old emergency room doctor was on his way home from a long shift in the ER when his car was T-boned at an intersection. He had a home, bank and investment accounts, safe deposit box, and other assets, several siblings, and an elderly mother who lived across the country. He had no Will and had done no planning. Ascertaining all of his assets and handling claims in the probate court were exceedingly difficult for his mother, who by law had priority for appointment as his personal representative. As there were siblings who did not get along, she determined that she could not turn over responsibility for settling her son's estate to anyone else. She relied heavily on the lawyer she hired, and the estate had high legal costs, which would have been significantly lower if the deceased son had specified his wishes in estate planning documents.

"I have set everything up myself and named beneficiaries so I don't need anyone's help."

Great, but remember, you do not know what you do not know. It is worth a few dollars in fees to have an estate planning attorney review your self-made plan. Consider the man who had a Will leaving everything to his children, which he thought was correct and sufficient. But, then he got married again and took title to his home, car, and bank accounts in joint tenancy with right of survivorship with his second wife. At his death, his wife got everything, his children got nothing, and his Will was meaningless. Based on his comments to his children close to the end of his life, it is clear that he believed the Will would prevail. Had he talked with the attorney who drafted the Will or another attorney qualified in estate planning, he would have learned that the titling of assets and beneficiary designations take precedence over the terms of one's Will.

The Last Minute Plan

The next story has a little different twist.

Richard's Story. Richard dealt in antique cars, and he attended a big show in Florida. When he got home from that hectic trip, he did not feel very well. He got in to see his doctor, who immediately put him in the hospital and told him to get his affairs in order. Richard did not have a lawyer, so his wife Susan went online and found an estate planning lawyer to speak with Richard. The attorney spoke with Richard on the phone and as Richard requested, showed up at the hospital a couple of hours later with a Will, power of attorney, health care power of attorney, living will, and cremation statement. The attorney went over the documents with him, he initialed and signed the pages from his hospital bed using a clipboard, and the attorney's staff, who had come along, witnessed and notarized his signatures. Richard died within twenty-four hours.

While the results from an estate planning standpoint were terrific, due to the fast action by the spouse and the attorney, the Will faced challenges from Richard's children from a prior marriage. They did not receive much, and the wife got most of the estate. It was an end-of-life document, and questions arose about his competency and undue influence.

The message here is very clear: "Don't forget to plan!" And, don't wait until you are almost comatose to do so. You might not find an attorney willing to meet you in intensive care.

Young Adults

Your adult children need to have these basic documents as well. Young adults increasingly have their own estates. By law, once a person reaches age 18 or is otherwise emancipated, parents and spouses have no legal right to make any decisions for him. It is often a nice gift, although perhaps not fully appreciated, for parents to pay for their children to have Wills, General Powers of Attorney, Health Care Powers of Attorney, and Living Wills. Young adults often do not think about their lives ending early or becoming incapacitated.

Ann's Story. A 23–year–old woman, Ann, was riding in the back seat of a car driven by a friend, along with the driver and three other passengers. All of them were intoxicated, and it was 3:00 AM. The driver wrecked the car, one passenger was killed, three were moderately injured, and Ann suffered a massive head injury leading to permanent disability. In order to make any but the most rudimentary medical decisions for her and in order to bring a personal injury lawsuit on her behalf, Ann's parents had to be appointed as her guardians and conservators by a court. It was an expensive and fairly grueling process for them to go through, and they were resistant to taking the step. Once they became Ann's guardians, however, doors for care and treatment, which had been closed to them and even previously unknown, were suddenly opened. If Ann had her legal documents in order – and of course been more selective about who was driving the car she was in – her parents would have saved months of time in getting her treatment, not to mention several thousands of dollars in legal fees.

If young adults also have their own children, a Will is essential so they can name the guardian and back-up guardians for those young children. There are usually four grandparents, two from the mother's side and two from the father's side. In the midst of the tragedy of the death or incapacity of young parents, their own parents could be embroiled in a massive court battle for the guardianship and conservatorship of the grandchildren. A great deal of additional strife and uncertainty can be avoided by all parents having Wills in which they name their choices of guardians and conservators for their minor children.

Remember to plan early and plan often.

3 PROBATE

So what is that thing called "probate" we hear about and why do we care? Probate is a court process. It's not just one thing. Think about when a person dies. If he holds the title to an asset (real estate, bank account, portfolio account, etc.), in his own name, with no beneficiary named, who has the legal authority over that asset? The correct answer is no one. A personal representative or executor must be appointed by the court, in a probate action, so that the personal representative can have legal authority over the assets owned by the decedent. Many people are under the incorrect belief that if they do not have a taxable estate, either at the federal or state level, their estates will not be subject to probate. This is simply not a true statement. The two situations, need for probate and having a taxable estate, have nothing to do with one another.

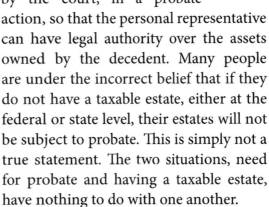

Probate assets typically do not include the following:

- real estate, bank accounts, and brokerage accounts owned with a spouse as community property with right of survivorship or with a spouse or another person as joint tenants with right of survivorship;

- any asset such as a life insurance policy, annuity contract, brokerage account, pension plan, 401(k) plan, or individual retirement account (IRA) in which a specific living person or charity is named as beneficiary;

- real estate for which a "beneficiary deed" is recorded, car titles or bank or brokerage accounts with "pay on death" or "transfer on death" ("POD" or "TOD") designations;[1] and

-assets owned in a trust.

That's a lot of assets not requiring probate. But, you still need a Will. Once the surviving spouse becomes the sole owner, she often won't deal with assets received in a community property with right of survivorship or joint tenancy with right of survivorship situation, leaving those assets subject to probate at her death. Those previously non-probate assets immediately become probate assets on the death of the joint owner unless additional planning takes place. And, as a reminder, assets such as these which do not go through probate are not affected by one's Will. Coordinated planning is a necessity.

The probate process differs somewhat in each state due to variations in state laws. There is a Uniform Probate Code; however, each state can make its own modifications to the uniform code. Older states tend to have more complicated procedures since their laws date back many years. Under the Uniform Probate Code, there is a formal process that requires

---

1 Check your state's laws to see if a beneficiary deed is authorized and for the specific rules regarding POD and TOD designations and naming beneficiaries on car titles.

a hearing before a judge in probate court, and an informal process that can be handled by the probate clerk, requiring no hearing. The choice between the formal and informal processes depends on the probate situation, whether there is a qualified person to start the informal process, the litigious nature of the various parties involved, the length of time since the decedent's death, and similar factors.

While many people wish to avoid probate of their estates at death, there are some benefits available in submitting a Will to probate. A key benefit in many states is that creditor claims against the decedent and his estate are barred after the passage of a few months from the date of notice of publication.[2] If there is a surviving spouse and the debts are joint or community liabilities, then such a bar may not do much for the surviving spouse. But, it can be very helpful to probate the Will of a professional such as a doctor, lawyer, accountant, etc., in order to bar malpractice-type claims and other personal claims, once the claims period of time has passed.

There are also many good reasons, if applicable, to want to avoid filing a probate. Some of these are as follows:

- In many states, attorney fees are based, by statute or by common practice, on the size of the estate and are usually stated as a percentage.[3] There are also executor fees and accounting fees incurred. Thus, probate can be an expensive proposition if it is needed (*see* above for discussion of probate and non-probate assets).

- Probate documents are public records, like most court-filed documents, so if anyone is interested in what the

---

2 Uniform Probate Code Sec. 3-803(c); *see* also, for example, Arizona Revised Statutes Sec. 14-3801(A) for a four month claims period.
3 California, for instance, Probate Code Sec. 10810 provides attorney fees of 4% on the first $100,000, 3% on the next $100,000, 2% on the next $800,000, 1% on the next $9,000,000, one-half of 1% on the next $15,000,0000, and as the court determines on estates exceeding $25,000,000.

Will says or what assets were owned by the decedent, she can find out by looking at the papers filed with the court in the probate. Large estates are likely to draw public attention. Very private individuals more likely than not will want their confidentiality protected in death just as in life.

- If real estate is owned by the deceased in her sole name in more than one state, or in a state other than the decedent's state of residency, there usually has to be a primary probate process in the state of residency and an ancillary probate in the other state where the real property is located. Often separate legal counsel is needed to represent the estate in the ancillary state. The costs become higher. Dealing with real estate in a foreign country becomes even more difficult.

- If any family member of the decedent is disaffected, disowned, does not like what he is getting from the estate, is otherwise disgruntled or just has a disagreement, having a probate matter open often makes it much easier for the displeased family member to bring his case before the court for inquiry, hearing, and maybe full-blown litigation. If no probate is needed, then that family member must be more active in voicing his gripes by starting his own court action to question the estate, the distribution plan, the administration, etc. While there can certainly be legitimate reasons to make such claims, many grievances have more to do with disliking one's siblings or step parent than having a valid concern. Remember that except for certain statutory laws for the protection of surviving spouses and minor children, each of us can do what we want with our assets at death: we can avoid the family entirely and leave it all to the "Flat Earth Society" or a meaningful charity, if we wish. We generally do not have "forced heirship" laws in this country.[4] We certainly can disown specific family members, including adult children. If a person is going to disinherit someone, particularly if the person typically would be expecting a part of the estate, then avoiding probate may be an appropriate choice. The disinherited person can always file a lawsuit to challenge a trust or a beneficiary designation, but that is a fairly difficult process. If a probate matter is opened with the court, however, it is much easier for the disaffected to step in with his claim.

- A business owner may wish to avoid the probate process with respect to the business. While the business should be able to continue operating during probate, in many situations, probate can complicate the business's functioning. The bank may call in the line of credit (which it can do on the death of the decedent as maker or guarantor anyway), suppliers could require COD orders only, and customers could become nervous, pulling their business away from the decedent's company. As mentioned above, not all probate laws are easy and straightforward, so a probate court could intervene in the business, appointing a receiver or requiring stringent accounting of business operations by the personal representative. All of these extraordinary situations will cost the estate more money in administrative fees and could actually reduce the value of an important estate asset, the business.

So, how does one avoid the need for probate? Review the list of non-probate assets above. A person can have a Will, but if titles to all assets are set up to avoid passage through the Will, either by operation of law[5] or through beneficiary

---

4 Forced heirship laws require one's estate to be left in a certain way, usually to male children. Such laws are most common in civil law and Islamic countries. Louisiana has a particular type of forced heirship that specifically benefits children under age 24 and incompetents at the time of a parent's death, which law may not be enforceable

5 *See* Glossary.

designation, then there will be no assets subject to probate. The problem with this circumstance can be that none of the terms of the Will will be applicable. For example, if a person holds his house with a second spouse as joint tenancy with right of survivorship or as community property with right of survivorship and is the first to die, and his Will says all of his assets will go to his three children at his death, the title on the house takes priority over what the Will says. The surviving spouse gets the house, and the children have absolutely no claim over the house, no matter what the Will says. As another example, parents will often make the mistake of naming their minor children as contingent beneficiaries on life insurance policies. They may have Wills which set up good trusts to hold the assets of their minor children, but the beneficiary designation will bypass the trust, so that the insurance proceeds will flow directly to the children despite the well-written trust. *See* discussion of conservatorship and of trusts for children in the following chapters. Thus, you need to plan, and your planning needs to include the expert services of an estate planning attorney.

4 REVOCABLE LIVING TRUST

Another popular and very workable way in most states[1] to avoid probate is to set up a revocable living trust. A revocable living trust is an estate and life planning tool. When you have a revocable living trust, it should be your primary estate planning document. Each spouse can have a separate trust agreement or a joint trust can be utilized. The revocable living trust has the following characteristics and performs the following functions. Note that these points will not all apply to irrevocable trusts.

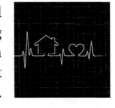

1. The person (or persons) who sets up the trust is called the trustor and can also be called the settlor, grantor, or "trust maker." In joint trusts by spouses, both are the trustors.

2. The person (or persons or institution)

---

1 Some states require judicial supervision of trusts created under Wills, so the revocable living trust is even more advantageous for maintaining privacy and avoiding court oversight in those places.

who is responsible for managing the assets of the trust and following the instructions in the trust for making distributions to or on behalf of the beneficiaries is the trustee. During his or her lifetime and competency, the trustor can be the trustee of the revocable living trust..

3. The people who receive distributions of income and/or principal from the trust are the beneficiaries. Generally, the primary beneficiary of the trust during the lifetime of the trustor will be the trustor himself. Other beneficiaries can be the spouse, children of the trustor, other relatives, charitable institutions, or anyone the trustor chooses.

4. The trust must hold title to all of the property formerly held by the trustor to be most effective. This ownership is accomplished by transferring title of titled property into the name of the trust (deeds to real estate, car and other vehicle titles, bank and portfolio accounts, certificates of deposit in banks, share certificates for stock holdings, etc.). Property held by the trustor outside of the trust may be subject to probate and/or conservatorship proceedings. This is the problem with omitting even one item of property. Some assets such as retirement plans cannot be owned by the trust during the trustor's lifetime, but the trust can be the beneficiary of those plans.[2]

5. The trust agreement will contain all dispositive provisions for the property during the lifetime of the trustor and at the trustor's death, including estate tax planning. This document will generally be used in lieu of the trustor's Will and will be the governing document for the trustor's estate. The trustor will have a new Will, known by its nickname as a "pour-over Will," which

2 There are tax implications regarding retirement plans which should be discussed with appropriate counsel.

will state that all of trustor's property not in the trust at the trustor's death is to be placed into the trust and administered according to its terms. In other words, the trust will be the beneficiary of the pour-over Will. It's important to have the pour-over Will so that the trustor does not die intestate, *i.e.*, without a Will.

6. Because the trust will own all of the trustor's property, at death, the trustor will have no property in his name for probate purposes. Thus, a major use of the trust is to avoid the necessity of probate. Property omitted from the trust will be given to the trust by the pour-over Will, but probate of that Will may be required.

7. Should the trustor become incapacitated or just unable to manage his financial affairs, there will be no need to have a conservatorship set up for the trustor because the trust will own all of the trustor's property. Thus, in life planning, a major use of the trust is to avoid the necessity of the expensive and time-consuming court procedure for an adult conservatorship. The trust is even more valuable to have in that situation.

8. For the trust to work best, the trustor must have no more than the probate limits of personal property (money, stocks, bank accounts, non-real estate assets), and real estate, held outside the trust. A probate limit is the value of property set by state law which, if owned solely by the trustor at death, does not require a probate action. The amounts vary by state.[3] Also, for the trust to work well to avoid the need of a conservatorship, the trustor must give a durable power of attorney to another person to enable the transfer of any remaining assets into the trust at the time of the trustor's incapacity.

---

3 As examples, in Arizona, the limits are $75,000 for personal property and $75,000 for real property. In Montana, the limit is $50,000 for personal property. In New York, it's $30,000.

9. If the trustor is also the trustee, then he (or a married couple) manages the assets in the trust as he has done prior to the transfer into the trust. The trustor/trustee can buy, sell, trade, spend, receive, and invest in the same manner as before the trust was set up. As long as the trustor is living, the trustor will have access to all of the income of the trust and pay taxes on it, and he may take principal out of the trust whenever needed or desired.

10. A successor trustee (one or more) should be named in the trust document to take over as trustee at the death or incapacity of the trustor. At that time, the successor trustee takes over and manages or distributes the trust assets according to the terms of the trust agreement. In the event the trustor is not able to decide upon a successor trustee or the list of named successor trustees has been exhausted, there are other ways to name someone as successor trustee. The last serving trustee can be empowered to name his successor; beneficiaries entitled to receive income from the trust can also vote for the successor; a trust protector can choose the successor trustee; or a petition can be filed with the court to request appointment of a successor trustee.

11. A person desiring to set up a revocable living trust should have the services of a licensed attorney who works in estate planning and understands estate tax issues. The cost of creating the trust, pour-over Will, and related estate planning documents as well as having assistance with asset transfers will vary depending on the complexity of the estate, the locale, the amount of property, and the level of customization of the documents.

Properly funded, the revocable living trust will not only avoid probate at the deaths of both the wife and husband, but also avoid the need in most cases for a conservatorship in the event there is disability before death. *See* the discussion of a conservatorship in Chapter 10. Proper funding means having titles to all assets held in the name of the trust or providing that title passes to the trust by beneficiary designation or by operation of law at the death of the trustor.[4]

How you hold title to an asset before it goes into the revocable living trust's name is important because the trust's ownership may or may not change that prior designation. It's impossible to continue ownership as "joint tenants with right of survivorship" in a trust because as an entity, the trust does not die in the way a person dies. But, under the laws of most states, deeding property held as joint tenancy with right of survivorship to an entity will break the "survivorship" feature and still result in a co-ownership of the property, most likely, tenancy in common between the trust and the other owner. It is very important to pay attention to how property is titled prior to it going into the trust. For example, you may have had some kind of contract with that co-owner to be sure if you were the first to die, that the property would belong to the surviving co-owner or vice versa.

There are presently nine community or marital property states plus Alaska which allows for the community ownership option. In a community property state, it is presumed that a married couple jointly owns their property unless they specifically take steps to hold it as "sole and separate" property or have inherited the property or acquired it by gift. The rules of each state are somewhat different, but the general idea is that each spouse has an undivided half interest

4 Note, however, that the ideal situation is to hold title in the trust name during life because it may be difficult to get title to all assets transferred if there is a disability. Durable powers of attorney work well in many situations, but not all IRA custodians, as an example, will allow a beneficiary designation change to be made with a power of attorney if the IRA owner is incapacitated

in community property. In common law states, there is no such presumption so how title to property is held must be specifically selected.

Here's some typical trust language for married persons on the subject: "The Trust Estate consists of the separate, joint, and community properties of the Trustors, all as designated in Schedule A, and the Trust Estate shall retain its character as the separate and community properties of the Trustors." There are various benefits connected with holding property as community, jointly, and even separately. Prior to transfer of your assets to your revocable living trust, it is important to identify how your assets are titled, make changes to the titling as desired, and then transfer the assets to your trust name.

Most revocable living trusts make reference to and have attached a schedule of assets owned by the trust. Just placing an asset on the trust's schedule is not enough to legally transfer title to the trust. Each asset must be dealt with separately. Real estate is deeded; vehicle titles are registered; bank and brokerage accounts must be specifically changed with forms provided by the financial institution; forms for insurance policies' ownership and beneficiary designations must be completed; stock shares should be reissued; and untitled assets should be transferred by assignment or similar document. It sounds like a complicated process; however, it is much easier while you are living and can identify and handle your own assets rather than thrusting that task on your fiduciary once you are incapacitated or deceased.

5 POWERS OF ATTORNEY, THE LIVING WILL, AND YOUR CHOICES

A nickname for the documents discussed in this Chapter is "Life Documents" or "Life Docs," for short. It is apt because these documents, if needed, are most often used during the client's lifetime for emergency purposes: financial or medical. These are extremely important documents to have, avoiding the need for emergency court proceedings, and the possibility of having someone declared incompetent or subjected to a commitment proceeding. In addition to the difficulties involved, these types of court proceedings are hugely expensive, compared to the cost of preparation of the "Life Docs." The documents expire at death, however, and are not a substitute for having a Will or a trust.

General Durable Power of Attorney

A power of attorney is a document you enter into as the "principal" in which you appoint another person or persons to act on your behalf, as your "agent" or as "attorney-in-fact." This power of attorney can be very broad and cover anything and everything which you might do for yourself, and in that situation, it is a "general" power of attorney. Or, the document can be limited in the scope of the granted powers to specific duties (a real estate transaction, child care during a week's vacation, access to an investment transaction, etc.), and then it is referred to as a "special" power of attorney. Most state laws provide that the ability of the attorney-in-fact to act under the power of attorney is extinguished when the principal (you) becomes disabled. Such termination is overridden by inclusion of a simple sentence, "This power of attorney shall remain in full force and effect notwithstanding the disability of the principal." Use of this sentence makes the power of attorney "durable." Durability is critically important because you want the general power of attorney to be used mostly if and when you become disabled.

So why do you need a general durable power of attorney? Well, you may be traveling abroad and want to empower your brother, sister, cousin, parent, or adult child to be able to act for you while you are away. More importantly, however, from a planning perspective, if you should suddenly become disabled and unable to manage your own affairs, or if you need assistance gradually over time due to advancing age, you need the general durable power of attorney appointing a responsible and trusted person to be able to write checks, pay bills, access your mail, and generally, speak for you. If you do not have a general durable power of attorney in place and you become disabled, an adult conservatorship must be set up for you, in court, at great expense and with court supervision and intervention.

Even if you have a revocable living trust, you need to have a general durable power of attorney in place. It will cover non-trust matters, such as pension plans and IRAs, mail, bank accounts not in the trust name, and a host of other situations which could arise. Again, the alternative to having a general durable power of attorney when you need it is a court process. Note that your attorney-in-fact will not be able to act regarding your trust matters unless you specially provide that authority, and even then, some financial institutions will not allow anyone except a trustee to access trust accounts.

The general durable power of attorney must also be sufficiently detailed in order to have it accepted by a bank or other financial institution. Even though it is a legal document, the law does not require acceptance of the power of attorney by a third party, so it must be written broadly and with a great deal of detail for it to be accepted for the needed purposes. The days of the one-page power of attorney are long gone. The document must be chock full of authorizations for as many activities by the attorney-in-fact that the average person may need to handle, from sale of real estate to banking, stock investments, and gifting. A typical, good general durable power of attorney should stretch to 8 or 9 pages or longer.[1] We suggest you check with your banks, IRA custodians, brokerage houses, and insurance companies for their acceptance of your power of attorney.

The general durable power of attorney should not have an expiration date on it. Since it is most beneficial as an emergency document, you don't want it to expire on the eve of you needing it. But, as a caution, these documents get "stale," so you cannot expect a financial institution, insurance company, title company or other entity to accept your power of attorney from your attorney-in-fact if it is considered too old. We strongly recommend that you update this important document every 3 to 5 years, or more frequently, so that it

---

1 A general power of attorney that simply states that the attorney-in-fact can do all things that the principal (*i.e.*, the person signing the document) could do is generally insufficient. The attorney-in-fact should be given very specific grants of power to be able to carry out the transactions needed to manage the principal's affairs if the principal becomes incapacitated. Banks, mortgage companies, and other institutions often will not accept "blanket" powers of attorney. Rather, specific authorization for the particular action contemplated must be clearly enumerated in the document.

will be an acceptable document whenever it may be needed. Updating means signing a new document which may include law changes, even if your attorney-in-fact and back-ups remain the same.

Be sure the person you have named is willing and able to act for you. You should ask him about his willingness to serve for you. Also note that co-attorneys-in-fact maybe named, and you should specify if they must act together or can act separately. Acting separately is usually more convenient.

Judy's Story. Judy developed emphysema from years of smoking. She also had some dementia but generally knew where she was and what was going on in her life. Her three children and she decided she should sell her large house and move to a senior care facility where she would have her own apartment. The children held her general durable power of attorney, dated thirteen years previously. When the house sold, the children presented the power of attorney to the title insurance company, and it was refused because the company policy was not to accept and such document more than six years old. Fortunately, Judy was capable enough to sign her own documents for sale of the house. Otherwise, the children would have needed to petition the court for temporary conservatorship papers in order to be able to sell the house for their mother.

Medical or Health Care Power of Attorney

Some states have specific language to use in the health care power of attorney, while the statutes in others are silent on the subject. Some practitioners combine the health care language in the general durable power of attorney. Either way, you also need a document in which you grant the authority to another person to make medical decisions for you in the event you cannot make them for yourself. Generally people name spouses and adult children in this agency role, but other relatives, close friends and attorneys may be designated as well.

Why do you need a health care agent? Won't the paramedics and emergency room doctors and staff keep you from dying if they can? The answer to that last question is yes, of course; however, once your condition is stabilized, there may be several decisions to be made about the next step. For instance, sometimes a stent is recommended for a stroke victim. But there are often complications immediately and later in utilizing a stent. You, as the patient, very well may be unconscious or at least not cogent enough to understand medical jargon or the description of your medical options. If no one is named in a medical power of attorney to make those decisions for you, then the alternative often will be someone seeking a temporary guardianship appointment [2]from the court, so that person can make medical decisions for you. The process of making health care decisions for you is obviously much easier, less expensive, and less grueling on family members, if you have had the foresight to sign a document appointing your health care agent (and one or more backups). Co-agents can also be named and be empowered to act jointly or separately, as you desire.

A number of other important decisions can be made in a medical or health care power of attorney. You can determine whether to have a voluntary autopsy, make organ and tissue donations, grant authority for certain people to obtain your confidential medical information, admit you for mental health diagnosis and care without a commitment hearing, set forth burial or cremation wishes, and in some states, make your declaration regarding use of life support when you are in the dying process. Let's look briefly at these additional decisions you should be making concerning yourself.

---

2 *See* Chapter 10 regarding guardianships. *See* also HIPAA discussion below.

Autopsy

An autopsy will normally be performed by the local medical examiner's office anytime a person has died alone or in a situation in which the cause of death appears questionable. So if that is your fate, you may not have any choice about the autopsy. Absent an official autopsy, there are often good, private reasons to have an autopsy. We know that various diseases and other ailments are passed genetically from one generation to another. Those with children may consider at least allowing their children to have an autopsy performed, if it is not already being done due to the circumstances surrounding the death, so that the children will potentially have information about their own medical possibilities. Further, there's a chicken or egg question which can possibly be resolved with an autopsy.

T-Bone Story. A man had a bang-up, T-bone car accident which was surprising for him, as a careful driver. It was determined at the scene that he had had a heart attack and consequently assumed that he ran a stop sign, causing the second car to careen into him. His widow was denied an accident claim recovery. She was distraught and did not think about having an autopsy, but an autopsy might have shown that the accident occurred at the fault of the second driver, which caused the fatal heart attack. Determining which event came first would have had important financial and emotional consequences.

Organ Donation

Some people are very much in favor of volunteering their bodies for organ and tissue donations, while others shy away from the concept. The health care power of attorney is a good space in which to express your wishes, because it is likely to be the document that will be on hand at the time you succumb. You can expressly choose to donate only certain organs and other body parts or make everything available. You may choose that your donation be only used for transplant and other therapeutic purposes or for "any legally authorized purpose," that could include being used as a cadaver in teaching or medical research. You may, on the other hand determine that you do not want your body used in any such manner and make that statement in your medical power of attorney. Or, you can let your agent make all of these decisions. For a final note on this topic, many people think that because of their older ages and other limiting factors, their bodies would not be useful for donation. As medical science progresses, however, more and more uses become available far beyond organ donations. For instance, burn victims can receive skin and connective tissues, which use may not be as age-dependent.

HIPAA Confidentiality Rights

Before the advent of the federal Health Insurance Portability and Accountability Act of 1996 ("HIPAA"), medical information was considered confidential, but the boundaries of that nondisclosure usually were determined by local custom, often at a doctor's office level. With the Act, the confidentiality and nondisclosure rules were codified nationwide. Now everyone who gets any kind of medical treatment is familiar with "HIPPA," as the anagram is often mistakenly written. With your own doctors' offices, you probably have had to provide lists of people who may have access to your records. In your medical power of attorney, you definitely need to provide that your medical agent has the right to know your medical condition by specifically referring to HIPAA. How else will that agent have the ability to make meaningful decisions about your treatment on your behalf? You definitely need to update your pre-HIPAA health care power of attorney.

Mental Health Care Agreement

Alzheimer's Disease and other illnesses which create symptoms of senility lead to mental health problems. We have all heard or experienced first hand the horror stories of unusual behavior exhibited by previously normal people who are in the throes of mental imbalances. Because we have the due process of law in this country, a person cannot be confined against her will without the right to a hearing and to confront her accusers. Someone exhibiting behavior which is bizarre and possibly dangerous to himself and others obviously needs diagnosis and treatment. If the afflicted party will not go willingly, then the alternative is a difficult court process called a "commitment hearing" in which medical and legal evidence is presented to the court for a determination as to whether the person should be involuntarily taken or "committed" to a hospital for diagnosis and treatment. This commitment process is understandable in our constitutionally-based legal system, but to subject Grandpa, who sits on his luggage waiting for the train fully dressed in the middle of the night in his bedroom, to a commitment hearing seems a bit draconian. In modern health care powers of attorney, Grandpa, as well as you, may choose to allow the health care agent to subject you to "level one" diagnosis and treatment voluntarily without the court hearing and court order. Because the health care power of attorney and the signing of the mental health portion is voluntary, due process rights are intact, particularly since, technically, Grandpa or you can revoke the voluntary agreement at any time. If Grandpa really is in advanced stages of Alzheimer's, then chances are that once he's diagnosed, he will not be in any condition to revoke the agreement, and treatment can proceed to keep him safe. Other issues regarding mental health, commitment proceedings, and patient rights are beyond the scope of this book.

Burial or Cremation Wishes

It used to be fairly typical to put burial wishes in one's Will, probably because it was an important document that would be kept safe. In our modern society, with families separated often by miles, the Will is often looked at much later after the funeral has occurred. That means that the Will may not be the best place to report your wishes. It is still important, however, to set forth your wishes and to state who has the legal authority to carry out your wishes. Here's why.

If you have specific wishes, you want someone to have legal authority to carry out those wishes provided it's not illegal to take a particular action. You would not want disagreeing family members to block your wishes or to create a family disturbance. By setting forth your burial or cremation wishes and naming someone to have legal authority to carry them out, you give your agent legal authority to act for you as your last wish. If you set forth what you want and your agent carries out your instructions, then no one has to make decisions for you, possibly agonizing over the decision and expense, and family members and others who were not part of the process will not have a legitimate subject for grievances.

Many states have specific rules about cremation.[3] Without a cremation statement signed by you, a mortuary may not be able to cremate you without the consent of all family members of equal consanguinity. Thus, if you do not have a spouse, all of your children would need to agree to your cremation. If you have no children, then all of your siblings would need to agree, and so forth. You cannot be certain that you could be cremated without your own personal statement, signed according to state law rules, to that effect.

---

3 For example, Arizona Revised Statutes Sec. 32-1365.01 states, "A legally competent adult may prepare a written statement directing the cremation or other lawful disposition of the legally competent adult's own remains…. The document shall be notarized or witnessed in writing by at least one adult…. It is not necessary for a crematory…to obtain consent or concurrence of any other person when it cremates…pursuant to instructions contained in a document that conforms to this section."

Living Will, Declaration or Advanced Directive

A living will, declaration of living will, or advanced directive provides your wishes regarding end of life care. These provisions can be contained in a medical power of attorney, but many states have statutory provisions which are usually set forth in a separate stand-alone document. This separation of provisions can be useful particularly if the patient is concerned about the withholding of medical treatment too soon. The living will is designed to be submitted by the health care agent, once the patient is in the dying process, an irreversible coma, persistent vegetative state, or similar description of a dying individual. Typical living will language provides for "comfort care," so you should not be fearful that you would be in pain if the living will were followed.

Some living will forms contain long lists of medical procedures that the signer either approves or disapproves. The concern about too much specificity is that the document probably will not keep up with medical technology. It will do little good to state that you don't want leeches used if that is no longer a medical procedure. It is better to follow the statutory form available in your state, and then specify additional wishes either in that document or in a separate statement to your health care agent. The separate statement would not necessarily be legally enforceable but would let your health care agent know your thoughts and individual philosophy regarding these important health care subjects.

What happens if you do not have a living will can vary from the practical to the absurd. In today's practice of medicine, dying patients are often too comatose to receive any significant nutrients other than hydrating fluids. Part of cancer treatment is to not give the cancer cells nutrients that would speed their growth. Pain monitoring will often result in the administration of increasing doses of morphine and similar drugs, until death occurs. The living will may really not have much impact.

On the other hand, without a living will with "do not resuscitate" language, emergency room personnel may not legally be able to stop reviving a heart attack patient without a clear pronouncement of death.

Mother's Story. The distraught daughter brought her 89-year-old mother in to the hospital because she was short of breath and experiencing intense chest pains. In the emergency room, the mother's heart stopped and the staff attempted to bring back the heart rhythm with the electric paddles 46 times before they were able to declare her dead. The daughter insisted on the repeated treatments and because there was no living will, there was no personal choice imposed over what the law required. A living will executed by the mother would have inserted some degree of sanity into that gruesome process.

Your decisions about these basic issues and the accompanying documents which give legal effect to your choices are needed by everyone who lives in this country, with no exceptions. Without these important documents, whatever state laws are in place, where you have your legal residence and any other place where you may pass away, and certain federal laws will control if you are unable to make your own decisions later and at your death. In most cases, exercise of your freedom of choice is essential. While the discussion of the details is long and may seem daunting, your decisions and the implementation of those decisions in the form of the Will and/or living trust, general durable power of attorney, medical or health care power of attorney, declaration/living will, and burial/cremation statement can usually be accomplished quickly by experienced legal counsel. These issues are too important for an untrained person, even an attorney working in other areas of law, to attempt on his own. Mistakes can be costly in many respects, either to repair or to handle in the aftermath.

6 TAX AND OTHER LAW CHANGES

The book entitled *General Explanations of the Administration's Fiscal Year 2013 Revenue Proposals*, referred to as the Green Book, dated February 13, 2012, contains many provisions for changes to the Internal Revenue Code of 1986 (referred to in this book as the "Code") which the Obama administration would like to see be enacted. Many of the favorable planning ideas contained in these chapters will be curtailed if the "wish list" provisions are passed into law. It is noted throughout these materials which planning tools may be at risk of disappearing, with passage of any such legislation. Many people took steps in 2012 to take advantage of the then existing tools, to avoid future elimination, with the hope that grandfathering would preserve those trusts and other entities put in place prior to 2013. At the time of this publication, it is unpredictable which changes, if any, will be enacted into the Code to alter some of the tax planning advice in this book. It is usually the case, however, that the sooner planning tools are implemented, the higher the likelihood of their success.

Other law changes besides the tax laws occur frequently. If you see something in the news about a law change which you think may be relevant, check with your advisors for potential impact to your plans. And, if you receive notice from your advisors about law changes, it's wise to schedule an appointment for a meeting or at least a phone call to see if the change is relevant to your circumstances.

7 GIFTING, GIFT TAXES AND GENERATION-SKIPPING TRANSFER TAXES

Gift Taxes

The gift tax is a federal tax to be paid by the person giving the gift, the donor, and is based on the net value of the gift at the time it is given. Gift taxes are levied only on completed gifts. Except for income taxes on certain types of gifts (generally IRAs and annuities) and on the income earned by the gifted property, 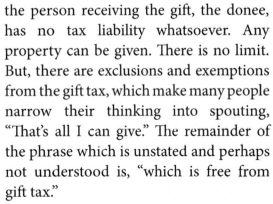 the person receiving the gift, the donee, has no tax liability whatsoever. Any property can be given. There is no limit. But, there are exclusions and exemptions from the gift tax, which make many people narrow their thinking into spouting, "That's all I can give." The remainder of the phrase which is unstated and perhaps not understood is, "which is free from gift tax."

The gift tax laws are as changeable as the estate tax laws, and while gift tax laws are often in sync with estate tax laws, that has not always been the case.[1] At the time of this publication, the gift tax exemption and the estate tax exemption are the same, are "unified," so that a person may make a gift of $5,000,000[2] tax-free during lifetime but will have in the process used up her estate tax exemption by the same amount. The unified exemption amount is one and the same, to be used in life or with transfers made after death. These two taxes are often referred to as "transfer taxes," as they tax the transfer of property from one person to another when made without consideration, or in other words, transfers which are not sales for a price.

There is also an annual <u>exclusion</u> from gift taxes, which in 2013 was set at $14,000 per year in net value of the gift, where it remains for 2014.[3] The exclusion is utilized by the donor for transfers of property made to each donee in a given year, so that the exclusion is per donor, per donee, per year. A wife and husband each has the annual exclusion, so a married couple can make a gift of $28,000 each year to one person, or many $28,000 gifts to multiple people each year. The donees are not limited to family members for purpose of the annual exclusion.

For example, a married couple wishing to make gifts to their two adult children and four adult grandchildren and a step-brother could give away tax free seven times $28,000 or $196,000 in one year without paying gift taxes or using any part of their gift tax exemptions. Come January of the following year, they could do it all over again.

In addition to the $14,000 exclusion, also excluded are

---

1 For instance, in the Economic Growth and Tax Relief Act of 2001, Congress set the lifetime gift tax exemption at $1,000,000, while providing that the estate tax exemption would rise over several years from $1,000,000 to $3,500,000. These laws changed substantially December 17, 2010 with the Tax Relief, Unemployment Insurance Reauthorization, and Job Creation Act.

2 This amount is increasing due to its being tied to inflation. In 2013, the amount was set at $5,250,000 per person and at $5,340,000 for 2014.

3 The annual exclusion is also tied to inflation, but it will only increase in $1,000 increments. It went to $14,000 in 2013 from $13,000 where it had rested for several years.

gifts of health care costs and educational expenses of tuition (but not room and board) which are made directly to the health care provider or educational institution, for the benefit of the donee, but which by-pass the donee's hands. Thus, grandparents who want to help with the education expenses of a grandchild, could pay his college tuition so long as their check was written to the college or university and not to the grandchild. They could then use their $14,000 exclusion each to write one or more checks to the grandchild to cover expenses for housing, board, transportation, etc.

Often people will have joint money and other assets which they give together, but if one spouse has sole and separate property she wants to use for gifting but wishes to exceed her annual exclusion amount, she may, with her spouse's permission, make a "joint gift." That means it's her property, but she employs not only her annual exclusion and exemption but also her spouse's annual exclusion and exemption. Joint gifts must be reported on the gift tax return, which is discussed below. Joint gifts must be made equally by the spouses and cover all gifts.

The catch, if you will, regarding the annual exclusion is that it must be for gifts of what is known as a "present interest" as opposed to a "future interest." In this context, future interest means gifts which will not be available to the donee until some future point, which is at least not right now. Most gifts to irrevocable trusts are treated as gifts of future interest because the trust beneficiaries must wait to receive any benefit.

As also discussed in Chapter 9 on Life Insurance, one method of qualifying gifts to irrevocable trusts for gift-tax-free treatment is to allocate portions of the gift to the trust beneficiaries and give the beneficiaries a limited right to withdraw the funds. It is usually hoped that no beneficiary will actually withdraw the funds or other assets. The assets can be then used for the purposes intended in the trust: to pay the premium on life insurance, make investments, own operating assets in an LLC or limited partnership, etc. The Tax Court case which approved this procedure involved the Crummey family, so the type of notice to be sent to trust beneficiaries concerning their withdrawal rights is nicknamed the "Crummey notice."

If a person makes a gift greater than his annual exclusion amount, then he uses up a portion of his personal exemption.[4] There is no choice to pay the gift tax in lieu of using up the personal exemption amount.

Any taxable gift, whether it uses part of the personal exemption or is large enough to require the payment of gift taxes, must be reported on a gift tax return, the IRS form 709, which is due by April 15 of the year following the calendar year of the taxable gift even if no payment of taxes is due. For example, a taxable gift made on March 1, 2012, should have been reported on a form 709 and the gift tax, if any, paid by April 15, 2013.

The gift tax return, IRS Form 709, is a combination of gift tax return and generation-skipping transfer ("GST") tax return. Regarding the gift portion of the return, information about the gift and the parties must be included on the return including the following: the description of the gift (*e.g.,* 5000 shares of Google stock), the donor's cost basis, the donee's name, the net value of the gift at the time of the transfer, and prior taxable gifts made by the donor (either in the form of exemption amount already used or gifts on which gift taxes were actually paid, but not annual exclusion gifts). Note that the donee receives the donor's cost basis (what was paid for it) in the gifted asset. This is referred to as "carry-over basis."

---

4 Remember that the <u>exclusion</u> is the once-a-year, per beneficiary right to give up to $14,000 tax-free. The <u>exemption</u> is your lifetime and at death $5,000,000 tax-free transfer amount. Both amounts will increase with inflation.

A family gifting program can accomplish many important goals. Often high net worth families whose estates clearly exceed the gift and estate tax exemption amounts are encouraged to make gifts to children and grandchildren to reduce their taxable estates by moving assets to others, trimming off appreciation on growth assets, passing income on to other taxpayers, and setting up GST tax exempt trusts for future generations (*see* discussion in next section). The best family gifting plans have purpose or missions, goals, and structure. Without legal consultation, gifting which is meant to be beneficial to the donees can backfire.

Kinzey's Story. When she turned 18, the first age of adulthood, Kinzey's parents gave her $20,000 tax free in cash and made a $500,000 contribution to a trust for her benefit. She was encouraged to go to college but chose to take a year off. In the next calendar year, they also gave her $20,000, the trust paid her $30,000 in net income earnings, and she did some traveling. By the next year, she had a similarly non-college-bound boyfriend, received $22,000 from the folks without strings attached, and an additional $30,000 in new income earnings from the trust. Kinzey never gave college another thought, spent her winters skiing in Telluride affording it by living in a house with 10 other people, and wiled away summers on the beach in Mexico. It was not clear what she wanted to accomplish, but she told her parents that she did not want to "live like them."

In the foregoing example, the parents were advised to begin a gifting program and were helped by legal counsel to set up the trust. But, other than tax savings, they had little discussion about what the program could mean for the future of their child.

Linda's and David's Story. Linda and David, on the other hand, in accumulating their assets over the years, had always been cautious about giving too much appearance of wealth to their three daughters. They wanted their children to be successful in their own rights by not having money doled out to them, and they did not want to set up a situation in which people, particularly boyfriend-types, "liked" their daughters because the parents were wealthy. When they met with their attorney, accountant, and financial advisor to set up a new estate plan, gifting was one of the topics, and serious discussion ensued. They discussed their desire for extensive charitable gifting and then made a sensible plan for gifting to the daughters. It included a requirement for community service before each year's gifts would be made and trust provisions that certain reasonable job earnings would need to be met before trust distributions could be made, with exceptions for illness, volunteer work, and community service or nonprofit employment. The hope, which has been realized, was that the daughters would be motivated to earn their own way, with the parental gifts and trust income being nice supplements.

Generation-Skipping Transfer Tax

The generation-skipping transfer tax ("GST" tax), besides being a mouthful of words, is the one of the four individual taxes (income, gift, estate, and generation-skipping transfer taxes) which most people don't know about. Even sophisticated individuals who have taken planning into their own hands often will miss the GST tax. It is a tax on distributions made to persons who are two generations below the donor or more than 37 years younger than the donor in the case of non-family members.[5] These include grandchildren, great nieces and great nephews, plus all of the great grandchildren, "great greats" and beyond. The tax is hefty: the rate is the largest estate tax rate in effect at the time, which could mean a whopping 40% or higher tax depending on future tax law changes.

---

5 Code Sec. 2651(d).

Fortunately, we each have an individual GST tax exemption amount, which has varied over time with the tax law changes. Now the GST tax exemption is the same sum as the estate tax exemption and is also adjusted each year for inflation. In 2014, the GST tax exemption for each donor is $5,340,000. But, unlike the gift and estate tax exemptions, the GST tax exemption is a separate exemption amount, thereby opening the door to wonderful planning opportunities.

The idea behind the GST tax dates back to when it was first introduced into the Code in 1976. At the time large families such as the Gallo family (winemakers) were reducing estate taxes on the whole pool of family wealth by skipping generations. Grandparents would leave wealth to grandchildren rather than to children, so that the funds would not be taxed in the children's estates. The first GST tax was cumbersome and did not do much to change the practice. In 1986, with amendments in 1987 and 1988, Congress revamped the GST tax provisions to create a fairly elaborate taxing scheme, with numerous rules affecting each type of gifting: direct transfers, transfers into trusts, trust distributions, etc. Fortunately, Congress also passed the per person exemption discussed above.

Each time a gift is made to an applicable donee, a gift tax return, the IRS Form 709, should be filed to allocate one's GST tax exemption. Direct, tax-free gifts have an automatic allocation of the GST tax exemption, but that means that you as the donor must keep track of the exemption amount used each time a gift is made, if you think you will exceed your GST tax exemption amount during your lifetime. Note that there is no annual exclusion for GST taxes, so if you make $14,000 per year gifts to your grand-children, you will have used a portion of your lifetime/at death unified GST tax exemption.

Charles's Story. Charles regularly made annual gifts to his children and grandchildren. The gifts to the grandchildren were made into trusts for his three granddaughters. Because those trusts included "Crummey" provisions and notices were given for the present interest requirement, he did not think he needed to file the Form 709. On consultation with his accountant and his tax attorney, he learned about the GST tax and the need to allocate his exemption. Even though the gifts to his granddaughters' trusts escaped gift taxes, the beneficiary withdrawal rights ("Crummey" notices) did not apply to the GST tax, so filing Form 709 was needed for each year in which he gave assets to a grandchild or to a trust for the benefit of a grandchild.

Dynasty Trust

Using one's GST tax exemption can be very powerful, particularly when the allocation or part of it is made to a long-term trust. The elimination of the Rule Against Perpetuities[6] by many states under their laws coupled with the GST tax exemption can allow creation of very long-term trusts benefiting multiple generations. This type of trust is often referred to as a "generation-skipping trust" or "dynasty trust." A dynasty trust, properly set up, is irrevocable and can accomplish the following for beneficiaries and for the trust estate:

---

6 The Rule Against Perpetuities is a common law rule which originated in 1682 with the Duke of Norfolk's Case in England to limit the duration of trusts. It was thought that long-term trusts which bound up real property and other assets would create an inappropriate situation for English lands and other assets. The basic rule was that a trust could not extend longer than the lives in being at the time the trust was created plus twenty-one years. The trust would terminate 21 years after the deaths of all beneficiaries who were living at the time the trust became irrevocable. This Rule against Perpetuities was codified into all U.S. state statutes in one form or another and followed for many years. Then, beginning in the late 1980's, several states began revising their statutes either to modify or eliminate the Rule Against Perpetuities. For instance, South Dakota, Delaware, Idaho, Pennsylvania, and Rhode Island allow trusts to run in perpetuity for liquid assets but not land; Kentucky repealed the Rule entirely; and Arizona imposes a 500 year maximum to the length of trusts organized under its laws. Colorado is 1,000 years, Florida 360 years, Nevada 365 years, Utah 1,000 years, Tennessee 360 years, and for real estate in Delaware, 110 years.

- Eliminate all estate taxes and generation-skipping transfer ("GST") taxes against the trust corpus for the duration of the trust, providing 100% growth (reduced only by income taxes) to the trust assets. Given that the maximum estate tax rate is 40% (depending on the law in effect at any given time), on a $20,000,000 trust corpus, contributed by a married couple, for example, that's $8 million which stays in the trust each generation rather than being spent on estate taxes.

- Provide beneficiaries of the trust with income, use of trust assets (consider the trust purchasing homes, cars, etc., making loans to beneficiaries, etc.), and use of trust principal, when needed for their lifetimes.

- Completely protect the trust assets from any claims of creditors of the beneficiaries, even in divorce or in bankruptcy.

- Provide payment for educational and medical expenses for all trust beneficiaries.

- And the list goes on.

To be its most effective, the Dynasty trust, which terms can be incorporated into your revocable living trust or life insurance trust, should have certain provisions. In order to provide the best creditor protection, the trust should empower the trustee with full discretionary authority and not require any distributions to the beneficiaries. Think about it: if the trustee is required to make certain distributions to a beneficiary who has creditor problems, then the creditors can seize those mandatory distributions. On the other hand, if the trustee has the authority to decide when, and if, to make a distribution to a beneficiary, the trustee may choose to withhold a scheduled distribution or make certain payments on the beneficiary's behalf to certain persons and not to others. Such preferential treatment by the trustee of the beneficiary's creditors, if the dynasty trust is worded well, will have no effect on the beneficiary, even if she is in bankruptcy where preferential payments to one's creditors is generally prohibited. Why is that? It's because the beneficiary does not a) own the trust; b) have any legal rights to demand distributions from the trust; and c) does not control the discretionary decisions of the trustee.

In order to keep trust assets from being included in a beneficiary's estate for estate tax purposes, the same types of provisions giving full discretion to the trustee will work well. Assets are included in a person's estate for estate taxes if the person during life can control the use of the property including to benefit herself.[7] If the beneficiary receives distributions from a trust which the trustee is required to make, those assets will be included in the beneficiary's estate. On the other hand, if the beneficiary can use or enjoy assets of the trust at the trustee's discretion, which assets remained owned by the trust, then those assets are not under the control of the beneficiary in the way contemplated by the Code and therefore, are not included in the beneficiary's estate for estate tax purposes. At the beneficiary's death, the assets stay in the trust's ownership under the purview of the trustee, and are available for use by the next qualifying beneficiaries in line.

Why would you want to deprive your children, grandchildren and subsequent generations of the freedom to decide how to use of your hard-earned assets? That's a question which some people raise, and it is a legitimate question. The answer has several obvious parts.

---

7 IRC Sec. 2036 reads, "(a) General Rule.– The value of the gross estate shall include the value of all property to the extent of any interest therein of which the decedent has at any time made a transfer ... by trust or otherwise, under which he has retained for his life or for any period not ascertainable without reference to his death or for any period which does not in fact end before his death– (1) the possession or enjoyment of, or the right to the income from, the property, or (2) the right, either alone or in conjunction with any person, to designate the persons who shall possess or enjoy the property or the income therefrom."

First, if your children can control their inheritances from you, those funds and properties will be included in their estates for estate tax purposes, risking shrinkage of assets by 40%, depending on the size of the estate and the laws in effect at the time of your children's deaths. What they would leave to their children of your assets could be only 60% of what they received from you, assuming either no growth or that your children consumed all of the growth. Other costs, such as probate of a child's estate, would also erode what is left to the next generation.

Second, if one of your children has a serious creditor problem (and remember that creditors can come in all shapes and sizes, from personal injury claimants to business creditors of your child or his spouse, to taxing authorities), then the child's creditors can readily seize all or part of the inheritance you have left to your child. There may be nothing left to go to your grandchildren. Thus, creditor protection is a primary advantage of the dynasty trust.

Third, in most states, inheritance is deemed to be the sole and separate property of your child with no right of a divorcing spouse to make a claim; however, once the property is in the hands of your child, she can decide or be convinced to put her spouse's name on those assets or to use the assets for jointly owned property. In a divorce, the spouse can claim his share of the assets you left your child. Since that divorcing spouse may or may not be the parent of your grandchildren, you have no guarantees that your grandchildren will end up with any of your inheritance.

The dynasty trust, however, if properly created, will not be subject to estate taxes at your child's death. Your child's creditors will not be able to seize any assets of the trust because the assets are owned by the trust and not by your child. And, unless your trust provides benefits to a child's spouse, that person will never have any legal claim to any of your child's inheritance left in the trust. At your child's death, the full trust corpus, which are the assets owned by the trust, will pass for the benefit of the next generation, beginning the trust's life cycle again.

You may include many, many provisions in your Dynasty trust which give guidance to the trustee. The trustee must act according to the terms of the trust for the beneficiaries and not for the trustee's own interest. You may provide that your trustee is to be sure each current beneficiary has a nice house which your child and her family may use rent-free for as long as she wishes, with the trust funds being used to pay the maintenance, upkeep, taxes, and insurance. Or, you may provide that the trustee loan trust funds to the beneficiary to buy her own house, so that the trust holds the mortgage and has a security interest in the house. That provision will protect the house from other creditor claims but give the beneficiary a sense of personal ownership. The trustee can be authorized to pay all education costs of a beneficiary, or you can give the trustee some discretion in deciding whether the educational expenses are worthwhile for the beneficiary or the trust estate. A degree in "basket weaving" may not be of real benefit to the beneficiary, but on the other hand, if your grandchild is an artist or simply needs to achieve a goal as a life challenge, the basket weaving degree may be just the ticket. Let the trustee decide, but give the trustee lots of directions and thoughts. You will want the trustee to stand in your shoes regarding such decision-making, either in being generous or in being stern, depending on your mindset. Your trust can and should be written to reflect your wishes.

The choice of states in which to set up the dynasty trust or rather to have a particular state's laws apply is an important consideration. As previously noted, Alaska, Delaware, Nevada, South Dakota, and Arizona have liberal laws allowing trusts to last for many years. Some of the states, however, distinguish between personal property and real property, disallow protection against divorcing spouses, etc., so it is important to analyze the trust's holdings to be certain the best state is selected for the assets held. And be sure there is a "flee" clause built into the trust document to enable the trustee or a majority of beneficiaries to change the applicable situs or jurisdiction of the trust.[8] To invoke application of a particular state's laws, a trustee or co-trustee from the chosen state usually must be named in the document and given administrative authority. The trust will go on for a long time so it is essential to have a mechanism to name successor trustees.

For a numerical example of the savings, a dynasty trust holding $2 million for 100 years, netting an annual rate of return of 3% (after income taxes and generous distributions of trust income to the beneficiaries) and payment of no estate taxes, will have a balance in excess of $100,000,000. The same $2,000,000 subject to estate taxes at the end of every generation of beneficiaries will yield approximately 18% of that figure, or approximately $18,000,000. $100,000,000 versus $18,000,000: which would you rather leave to your future descendants? This type of specific planning can avoid the dissipation of family fortunes.

Be aware, however, that part of the tax reform plan set forth in the Green Book limits the term of any trust to a ninety (90) year term for tax purposes.

---

8 A problem exists, however, if the movement to another jurisdiction or any other change in the trust could cause a material or substantial change, a "constructive addition," in the interests of the beneficiaries. This would lead to a violation under IRC Sec. 2041(a) (3) subjecting the trust to the generation-skipping transfer tax, where none would have otherwise been owed.

8 ESTATE TAXES

Estate taxation has been a difficult topic to write about until recently because the law was in a state of flux. Congress and the administration in the last hours of January 1, 2013 acted to permanently set the gift and estate tax exemptions at $5,000,000, annually adjusted for inflation, rather than sending us back to the dark days of the mere $1,000,000 exemption.[1] What does all of this mean exactly? Primarily, such a large exemption amount means that the vast majority of Americans do not need to even think about estate tax planning (unless they live in states that have state estate taxes with lower exemption amounts). Only those wealthier married couples holding assets worth in excess of $10,000,000 (adjusted each year for inflation) between them need to be concerned about the federal estate tax.

---

1 American Taxpayer Relief Act of 2012, PL 12-240, 126 Stat. 2313, actually signed January 2, 2013.

The estate tax is a tax on the transfer of assets at a person's death. It is the estate which has the tax liability. This should not be confused with an inheritance tax, which is a tax imposed on the wealth that a person receives by devise or bequest, and the recipient is responsible for the tax. The federal government only has an estate tax, and many states which used to have inheritance taxes have changed those in favor of the estate tax. This discussion will focus on the federal estate tax, but the reader is encouraged to learn what laws your state has with respect to estate taxes or inheritance taxes.

The federal estate tax must generally be paid within nine months after the death of the decedent. A federal estate tax return, IRS Form 706, is due at that time, although an extension may be granted for filing the return. There is no extension for payment of the taxes. Penalties and interest are levied if the payment or filing is late. The tax is based on the net value of all estate assets as of the date of death, less certain allowable exemptions. The number of estate tax returns filed each year has been decreasing over the last decade, most likely due to the increase in the personal exemption amount. With fewer than 10,000 returns filed in a given year, the likelihood of the estate tax return being audited or at least reviewed increases significantly. The number of filings, however, may increase now with the advent of "portability" which allows the surviving spouse to file a return to preserve his or her rights in the deceased spouse's unused exemption ("DSUE") amount. See below for more discussion.

Assets in one's taxable estate include any and all property owned in some fashion by the decedent: real estate (even that which is jointly owned and may pass to a surviving owner), stocks and bonds, brokerage accounts, notes, cash, bank accounts, life insurance policies on the decedent's life over which she had "incidents of ownership,"[2] jewelry, collectibles,

---

2 *See* Code Sec. 2042(2); Regs. Sec. 20.2041-1. Incidents include the ability to change the

cars, art, other personal effects, annuities (if there is a death benefit or additional payments to be made after death), tax refunds due but not yet received, receivables, partnerships, sole proprietorships, and other business interests, individual retirement accounts (IRAs), pension and profit sharing plan accounts, 401(k) accounts, powers of appointment to one's self, estate or creditors, etc.

The deductions available to the estate include expenses of last illness, funeral and burial expenses, accountant fees, attorney fees, charitable gifts, mortgages on property, debts of the decedent which become debts of the estate, claims against the estate and costs of defending against such claims, costs of property upkeep while the estate is being administered, and similar items, and the marital deduction.

The last deduction, the marital deduction, is very important in planning. It is a deduction against the taxable estate tax for the value of all assets which pass to the surviving spouse. It is a 100% deduction. For example, a married man leaving his estate of $100 million in its entirety to his wife knows that his estate will not pay any estate taxes whatsoever at his death because the amount left to the wife, the $100,000,000, is a full deduction, leaving him with a taxable estate of zero. The wife's estate, however, at $100 million plus the wife's own net worth will have a serious estate tax problem at her death regardless of the amount of the estate tax exemption. Thus, a couple with a combined estate of $100 million needs extensive estate and estate tax planning to minimize as much of the 40% estate tax at the death of the survivor as possible.

A potential benefit to beneficiaries of an estate or revocable living trust is the possibility of a step-up in cost basis as provided in Code Sec.1014. The estate's or beneficiary's new cost basis in each asset will be its fair market value on the date

---

beneficiaries on the life insurance policy, borrow from the cash value, modify the policy in any manner, transfer ownership of the policy, use the policy as collateral for a loan, etc.

of the decedent's death. If the property has gone up in value since the decedent acquired the property, the beneficiary gets an added benefit with the higher cost basis. A sale of estate property with an increased cost basis will result in no taxable gain for income tax purposes. The opposite can be true, as well, with a decrease in value. No loss can be taken on sale.

Some people wish to leave property for their spouses to use but want to control the ultimate distribution after the spouse's death. In the Economic Recovery Tax Act of 1981, Congress approved the concept of the Qualified Terminable Interest Property Trust, or "QTIP" Trust for short, enabling both the having and eating of the cake. The QTIP Trust must provide solely for the surviving spouse and distribute all net income earned from its assets to the surviving spouse. But, it qualifies for the 100% marital deduction against estate taxes for the value of all assets transferred to the QTIP Trust. The surviving spouse can be the Trustee of the QTIP Trust, and these provisions will still work. Further, the deceased spouse can direct in the terms of the QTIP Trust how the property is to be distributed at the death of the surviving spouse. The funds may go to the children of a first marriage by the deceased spouse, a favorite charity, etc., and the surviving spouse has no authority over that distribution. As with other property qualifying for the marital deduction on the death of one spouse, the QTIP Trust property is included in the taxable estate of the surviving spouse, but the estate taxes attributable to the QTIP Trust assets are to be paid from the QTIP Trust property.

When the surviving spouse is not a U.S. citizen (referred to technically as an "alien"), a special trust called a Qualified Domestic Trust or "QDOT" must be established in order for the deceased spouse's estate to qualify for the 100% marital deduction for assets passing to the surviving alien spouse. The purpose of the QDOT and its elaborate rules is to insure that the estate taxes are ultimately paid on the assets of the

QDOT either as received by the surviving alien spouse or at his death. The QDOT must have a qualifying U.S. trustee. Further distributions of principal during the lifetime of the surviving alien spouse are subject to estate tax at the time the distributions are made. Income must be distributed to the surviving alien spouse, similar to the QTIP Trust rules discussed above.

The estate tax rates have varied over time, depending on changes in the law. The rate of tax to be paid, once the exemption amount has been exceeded, in effect beginning in 2013 is 40%. The rate with the $1 million exemption from the 2001 laws was 50%, with a surplus of an extra 5% on any taxable estate in excess of $10 million, for a maximum tax rate of 55%. The tax rates are high enough clearly to make some planning, either for payment of the tax or for reduction of the taxable estate, an essential piece of estate planning for those people with taxable estates.

The way the estate tax amount is calculated is interesting and gives rise to nomenclature which seems unusual to the uninitiated. On the Form 706, which you can view online at the website for the Internal Revenue Service, the various assets of the estate are listed on schedules with their values determined as of the decedent's date of death. Those schedules are added up, netted against deductions, and an amount of the gross estate value is carried back to the first page of the return to line 1. Then, lifetime taxable gifts are added back in to the value of the estate on line 2. This adding back is meant to insure that, while gifts are not part of the estate for present estate tax purposes, the estate is taxed at the higher brackets of the estate taxes. For example, if the taxable lifetime gifts are taxed at 18% and 20%, and are not added back into the estate, then the final estate taxes will include more of the estate in those lower brackets than allowed. So, the taxable amount of gifts must come back into the estate to calculate the estate tax.[3]

The estate tax is calculated on the net taxable estate. On a net taxable estate of $7,200,000, the tax is $2,825,800, representing a run up the estate tax brackets to the highest rate of 40%. From this gross tax amount two items are deducted: 1) the amount of any prior gift taxes paid since the prior gift was included in the estate for calculation purposes (assume none in this example); and 2) the exemption amount which is set forth in the form of a credit against the tax. The credit is the amount of estate taxes on the exemption amount. In this example we used the 2013 exemption of $5,250,000, so that the tax at the 40% top tax rate is $2,045,800. The credit to be applied to the tax is reduced by any prior credit used in lifetime gifts. Once the available credit is deducted from the gross amount of the tax on the estate, the resulting number is the amount of estate taxes which are due.[4] In this example, the tax to be paid is $780,000, leaving a remaining net estate after taxes of $6,420,000.

It is the responsibility of the executor or other person in charge of the decedent's estate to obtain the value of the assets, file the estate tax return, and pay any estate taxes due. If the estate assets total less than the unused exemption amount of the deceased, then no estate tax return needs to be filed, generally. The IRS will review the return, contact the responsible person if there are questions, and issue a closing letter if no changes are needed. The IRS becomes more

3 Note, however, that if gift taxes are paid on the taxable gifts, those taxes are excluded from the estate tax calculation, so that payment of gift taxes during life can be one way to reduce the overall estate tax burden at death. The gift may be included back in the estate but not the tax paid. On the other hand, there is no deduction for any tax purposes for the amount of gift or estate taxes paid by an estate.
4 As a result of the use of the exemption amount in the form of a credit against tax, in planning documents and in discussions, the "bypass" or "B" trust is also referred to as the "credit" trust or the "credit shelter" trust. What goes in this trust is an amount of the deceased spouse's estate equal to the deceased spouse's remaining exemption amount, in order to preserve the exemption and not have it be lost when the surviving spouse dies. See discussion below, however, for the newly created "portability" concept for the surviving spouse's estate.

involved only if there are serious disputes about the assets listed, the values given, or the expenses deducted.

It has been a long-standing tenet for estate planning attorneys to be sure to put bypass, A-B, credit, or credit shelter trust language in any Will or revocable living trust document to preserve the deceased spouse's estate tax exemption amount so that the property would not be included in the estate of the surviving spouse. Previously only the bypass trust provisions were available to preserve the deceased spouse's exemption and still provide benefits to the surviving spouse.

The bypass trust is designed to hold the deceased spouse's separate property and share of marital property up to her exemption amount or value of the assets, whichever is less. The assets in the bypass trust will not be included in the surviving spouse's estate for estate tax purposes even if there is appreciation. The surviving spouse is often named as the trustee of the bypass trust. The surviving spouse usually is entitled to receive the net income from the trust and can use principal when the ascertainable standard of health, education, maintenance and support ("HEMS") is met. A "5x5"[5] power can also be provided. Children of the deceased spouse may also be beneficiaries of this bypass trust. At the surviving spouse's death, the trust will be distributed according to its terms, usually to the offspring of the deceased spouse. The trust becomes irrevocable at the deceased spouse's death.

Mary's and Bob's Story. Mary and Bob had built a comfortable estate worth $7,000,000, $1,000,000 of which was Mary's sole and separate property which she inherited from her parents. The remaining $6,000,000 was jointly owned between Mary and Bob. Their revocable living trust provided that a deceased spouse's separate property and half

---

5 The surviving spouse is entitled to take the greater of $5,000 or 5% of the value of the trust principal each year without a showing of need.

of their joint marital property would be transferred to the bypass or credit trust, up to the estate tax exemption amount available at the death of the first spouse. Mary died suddenly.

Following the trust agreement terms, Bob transferred Mary's inheritance and half their joint property to the credit trust, for a total of $4 million, which was less than the exemption amount available to Mary. Bob was the trustee. He continued to invest the funds, took the net income for himself, and allowed the principal to grow. He did not take out the 5% per year which he could have under the 5x5 power because he did not need it and it was not necessary for estate tax planning. At Bob's death, he had a $3,000,000 estate which was not subject to estate tax. If the whole estate had gone directly to Bob at Mary's death then at his death in 2013, the taxable estate of $7,000,000 would have been taxable to the extend it exceeded his $5,250,000 exemption. At the 40% estate tax rate, $700,000 of estate taxes would have been due. Use of the credit trust for Mary's share of the estate saved the family $700,000 in federal taxes.

"Portability" is a concept which was introduced into the Internal Revenue Code, at Sec. 2010(c)(5), with the 2010 tax act.[6] Previously only the bypass trust provisions were available to preserve the deceased spouse's exemption and still provide benefits to the surviving spouse. With the 2010 act, such provisions are no longer necessary in estate planning documents in order for the surviving spouse's estate possibly to be able to use the deceased spouse's exemption. This new concept in the law is a major breakthrough, particularly for married couples who have not done proper planning prior to the first death. Having portability as part of the law, however, does not eliminate the need for good planning and for the insertion of estate tax savings devices into one's documents.

---

6 The Tax Relief, Unemployment Insurance Reauthorization and Jobs Creation Act of 2010, PL 111-312.

There are several rules connected with portability which can make the situation much more complicated. First, the surviving spouse cannot have remarried if his estate administrator wants to use the portability provisions from his first wife for tax savings. Further, in order to claim portability in the second spouse's estate, there must have been a timely filed estate tax return at the death of the first spouse, even though no taxes were due. This estate tax return is necessary to make the election to qualify the surviving spouse's estate for portability. Portability is only a federal tax provision and does not apply to any state estate taxes. Thus, careful planning is still needed to take advantage of any state estate tax exemptions. With no planning and without meeting portability requirements, the deceased spouse's exemption would be forfeited at the death of the first spouse, leaving the surviving spouse with only one exemption.

Cyclist's Story. The 50-year-old woman was very athletic and engaged in her morning bike riding ritual in the summer of 2011. She had 20 minutes to go on her ride before returning home to her husband and 3 minor children. She was chugging nicely up a hill with measured breathing, a light sweat, and endorphins rushing. Suddenly without warning, she felt a pressure followed by a sharp pain in her back and chest. She collapsed off her bike, gasped and died of a massive coronary. She and her husband had recently sold a successful business for $7 million and with other assets they had a net worth of $9,000,000. They figured it was time to do some estate planning and had an appointment with a tax lawyer in a couple of weeks. Without portability, the husband would only have his exemption amount of $5,000,000 (plus the inflation adjustment). If he died before the end of 2012, he would have a taxable estate of $4,000,000, taxed at 35% for roughly a $1.2 million tax bill. The lawyer he consulted with correctly made the call that the portability election was critical to make, to preserve the deceased wife's exemption amount of $5,000,000 by filing an estate tax return although no taxes were due (her portion of the estate was $4,500,000, less than the $5,000,000 and subject to the 100% marital deduction). With her exemption in place, the husband's $9 million estate (assuming no growth) may not be subject to any tax with his $5 million exemption. While it would have been far better for this couple to have engaged in planning in advance of the wife's sudden death, portability will preserve a large amount of the estate for the children.

There are several reasons not to rely on portability alone. It does not apply to the allocation of the deceased spouse's generation-skipping transfer tax exemption. The deceased spouse's exemption amount is "frozen" at his date of death. Funds in a bypass trust can appreciate in value without further estate tax. And, unlike with the use of the bypass trust, there is no asset protection for the assets in the hands of the surviving spouse. Nevertheless, portability is an important tool for use when couples have not planned and can no longer engage in the planning process.

9 LIFE INSURANCE

Life insurance on your life, your spouse's or business partner's life, and even on the lives of your children, can provide many benefits which often cannot be duplicated in any other manner using the same money. The uses are broad and varied.

Sufficient life insurance is an essential feature of a well-balanced estate portfolio. Life insurance can serve many purposes, and the types of life insurance products that should be purchased will depend on the needs of the individual. To do a good job for her clients, a life insurance agent must be well-versed in product information, the needs of the client, financial planning methodology, and estate tax planning devices. The following is a brief list of some of the more common uses of life insurance in estate planning. The list is not intended to be exhaustive, as each person's situation may generate new uses for life insurance.

1. **Provide cash to the estate to pay estate taxes.** With the tax law changes in the 2012 American Taxpayer Relief Act ("2012 ATRA"), Congress made the per person estate tax exemption amount of $5,000,000 permanent and indexed it for inflation. The downside was that the Act also increased the federal estate tax rate to forty percent (40%) from thirty-five percent (35%). In a taxable estate situation, estate taxes are due within 9 months of a person's date of death. Often life insurance proceeds are the only source of cash readily available to pay the tax liability. A "fire sale" liquidation of estate assets may be necessary if there are insufficient life insurance proceeds or other cash, and that quick sale of assets can create major losses of revenues and financial hardship to the family of the deceased. Life insurance, if owned by an irrevocable trust or another individual (preferably not the spouse of the insured), is an asset which can benefit the estate for payment of taxes or provide cash for other purposes, without being included in the estate for estate tax purposes. Even for estates that do not have estate tax liabilities, life insurance proceeds usually are essential to provide operating funds to the family at the time of the insured's death, for paying the mortgage, other debts, child care, attorney fees, probate costs, accounting fees, and living expenses.

The recent liberal estate tax law changes have made many people more complacent because they have no liability for estate taxes. The concerns over the financial well-being of one's estate, however, should still exist: many states are taking steps to increase their revenues with state estate tax laws, replacing losses to state coffers due to federal law changes; the basis step-up may be phased out and eliminated for many estate assets substituting income tax for estate taxes if and when assets are sold; and due to sizable revenue losses if there are limited federal estate taxes, it is likely that Congress will institute different kinds of taxes which in their own way can cause depletion of estate or beneficiary assets. Worries over these and other concerns can be reduced with a proper level of life insurance for your estate.

2. **Reduce the size of the estate.** Not only are life insurance proceeds excluded from the estate for estate tax purposes if owned outside the estate of the insured, but the premiums paid for the life insurance are generally removed from the estate for estate tax calculation purposes. Other property transferred outside the estate gives no further benefit to the estate or its beneficiaries, whereas life insurance proceeds can be utilized by the estate in the future through properly drafted language in a life insurance trust.

The person who "self-insures" could be missing a valuable investment opportunity. Self-insurance merely means that the individual accumulates the same amount of money in his estate as the insurance policy would provide. The self-insurance proceeds, however, in most cases will be included in the estate for estate tax purposes or if excluded, at a higher the gifting and tax costs are higher, whereas the life insurance investment can be removed from the estate by transferring the policy to a life insurance trust or having the trust purchase the life insurance directly. Further, the proceeds of life insurance policies are not subject to income taxation unlike most of the investment portfolio earnings of a self-insurer would be. Under today's highest income tax laws, the self-insurer must make potentially an additional 43.6% in income or growth (taking federal taxes only into account) to equal the income tax-free proceeds provided by a life insurance policy.

3. **Asset replacement.** Many people utilize charitable remainder trusts to remove appreciating assets from their estates for charitable gifting purposes, to avoid capital gains taxes, and to reduce the size of their estates for estate tax purposes. Once an asset is placed in a charitable remainder trust, however, it no longer easily benefits the family of the trustor. With insurance coverage, the trustor can provide for "asset replacement" with an insurance policy payable to his heirs at death, without additional tax cost. With the life insurance proceeds, the family can either purchase the asset

from the charitable remainder trust or enjoy the benefit of the liquid cash as part of their inheritance from the senior family member.

4. **Business Succession planning.** Life insurance is very useful in enabling a business succession plan to be funded for buy-out purposes without having to utilize company assets or company profits. The family of the deceased owner similarly benefits in that the funds are readily available, and the payment is not dependent on the risk that the business will fail without the deceased at the helm. The remaining or new owner will have a business which is not saddled with debt owed for the deceased owner's interest, and further, will not have, as is often the case, the family members of the decedent as unwanted "partners."

5. **Alternative retirement planning.** A life insurance product which generates a significant cash value over time can be used to provide tax-free retirement funds, without the onerous taxation usually connected with tax-qualified retirement plans. The cash value can be borrowed by the owner, and if the funds are not paid back, the life insurance proceeds payable on death simply will be reduced by the loan amount and a usually modest interest rate. There will be no requirement for paying back the loan.

6. **Life insurance for generation-skipping transfers.** A generation-skipping trust, which will last for many years and may create a family dynasty, can be funded economically with life insurance, thereby keeping the transfers within the senior generation's exemption amount for generation-skipping transfer tax purposes, yet allowing for wealth accumulation over many subsequent generations. *See* Chapter 7 for further discussion of the generation-skipping transfer tax and planning with multi-generational trusts. For example, a two million dollar policy paid at the insured's death to a life insurance trust with dynasty provisions can conservatively grow to be $100 million or more in 100 years.

7. **Wealth replacement following long-term care costs.** Many people fail to plan for long-term care expenses by purchasing long-term care insurance, or they do not qualify for the insurance due to pre-existing conditions. Often, a life insurance policy can be issued for an individual who would not qualify for long-term care coverage. Pre-existing conditions can often expire several years after recovery. The life insurance can be used after death to replace money and other assets expended in caring for a deceased insured who accumulated expenses of long-term care prior to death. This methodology can benefit the surviving spouse, so that he is not destitute, and the children who may have become parental care-takers.

8. **Loss of Income or Services.** Insurance is vital in protecting against the loss of income of a working spouse. And, do not forget about its use in replacing the services of a stay-at-home parent as well. Paying for outside help to replace the child-caring and homemaking services of a deceased parent can be quite costly. Any couple with minor children should have some life insurance coverage on both parents, not just the major income-producer.

Note that just as laws change and Wills and trusts need to be reviewed and amended from time to time, your life insurance policies should be reviewed and analyzed with some frequency. Every five to seven years is recommended. If you regularly work with your agent, then she is probably reviewing the policies for you, but if you no longer work with the selling agent, take those old policies to a good professional agent to see if they are still in force and performing well to give you the vital life insurance coverage you expect.

Irrevocable life insurance trust

The irrevocable life insurance trust ("ILIT") has been a frequently used and valuable tool of estate and estate tax planning for decades.

All assets owned by a person are included in measuring the size of her taxable estate. The death benefits on any life insurance that she owns, because she retains the power to change the beneficiary and other "incidents of ownership," are also included in her taxable estate (even though the proceeds do not become available until after death). Thus, life insurance can significantly inflate the size of the taxable estate without providing any economic benefit to the insured during her lifetime. It is for this reason that placing life insurance in an ILIT is a popular tax-savings mechanism.

A properly constructed ILIT will avoid the inclusion of the life insurance proceeds in a person's taxable estate. This tax treatment is possible because when life insurance is owned by an ILIT and the insured retains no control after its inception, the trust is treated as a separate person for estate tax purposes. At the time the trust is written, the insured as trustor will be able to choose the trustee, the beneficiaries, and the terms and conditions by which the trustee determines when to make distributions from the trust to the beneficiaries. Once the trust is created, however, it becomes unamendable and irrevocable. The named trustee will have full management authority over the policy and its proceeds.

Once assets are transferred to any irrevocable trust, that transfer is irrevocable or irreversible, in most situations. Subject to applicable laws, the transfer removes the transferred asset from the estate of the transferring party. The transfer, however, is a "taxable transfer" for federal gift tax purposes, which means that it is subject to federal gift taxes. As further discussed in Chapter 7 concerning gift taxes, a person must first use up his lifetime exemption from gift taxes (now $5,000,000 adjusted for inflation) before he is liable to pay any money for the transfer. With the ILIT, there are some planning tools discussed below which can be used to avoid or reduce gift taxes.

For the best result, the trust should be established before the insurance policy is obtained. That way, the trustee can be the applicant on the life insurance application. If, on the other hand, the insured takes out the policy and then transfers it to the trust, the estate tax exclusion benefits discussed above will only become available three years after the transfer of the policy to the trust. Looking from the other way, if the insured person dies within three years of transferring a life insurance policy to an ILIT, the proceeds are still included in his taxable estate. If, however, the ILIT obtains the policy directly at the beginning, the insured has never owned it, never transferred it, and the tax protection offered by the trust is immediately available. The transfer of money or other property (except the life insurance policy) to an ILIT, whether to pay for the premium or for other purposes, is not subject to this 3-year inclusion rule.

Another important element of the life insurance trust is the manner in which premiums are paid. In order to pay the premiums each year, someone, usually the trustor as the insured, will have to contribute funds to the trust. It is important that the funds be paid first to the trust and that the trustee, in turn, uses the funds to pay the insurance company for the policy premium. Although paying the premiums in this manner may seem like a cumbersome formality, it is an important factor in complying with the tax laws governing ILITs.

To reiterate, each time someone, whether it's the trustor or another person, makes a contribution to the irrevocable trust, that person will be making a taxable gift to the trust. There are several important exclusions and exemptions regarding application of the gift tax rules, however, and with proper planning, those can be utilized to reduce or eliminate the gift tax burden of funding the ILIT. There is the donor's lifetime exemption for gifts, which usually is the same amount as the estate tax exemption. It is important to remember that each gift made under the gift tax lifetime exemption not only exhausts the donor's lifetime exemption for gift taxes, but it also exhausts an equal portion of her lifetime exemption from estate taxes. Consequently, knowledgeable planners look for ways to avoid the use of the lifetime exemption as much as possible, except for well-planned transactions.

In addition to the lifetime exemption, there is the "annual exclusion." The annual exclusion provides that the first $14,000.00[1] that each donor ($28,000.00 per married couple) gives to a particular donee in a given year is excluded from gift tax calculation and does not use a portion of the donor's lifetime exemption from estate and gift taxes. In order for the annual exclusion to apply, however, the gift must be a gift of a "present interest." Yes, a gift is a present, but the "present" referred to in this case is about timing. The alternative to a present interest is a future interest, which means that a gift recipient cannot enjoy the gift now, in the present time, but rather must wait for some point in the future. Only a present Interest gift qualifies for the annual exclusion.

Generally, a contribution to a trust on behalf of a beneficiary is not a present interest because the trust terms limit the beneficiary's immediate access to the gift. A contribution to a trust when the trust terms provide the beneficiary with a limited right to withdraw the contribution, is, however, a gift of a present interest. Therefore, by giving your beneficiaries limited withdrawal rights over trust contributions (these withdrawal rights are sometimes referred to as "Crummey powers," named for the court case[2] approving this gifting technique several decades ago), and formal notice each time a withdrawable contribution is made, contributions to the trust at or under the donor's annual exclusion amount will not have a gift tax cost. They will qualify as present interest

---

1 The Code at Sec. 2503 provides that the annual gift exclusion per person is $10,000, indexed for inflation in $1000 increments. Since the modifications of that Code section made in 1997, the annual exclusion increased by $4000 to $14,000 in 2013.
2 *Crummey v. CIR*, 397 F2d 82 (9th Cir.) 1968.

gifts. The size of the annual insurance premium may dictate how many beneficiaries are given Crummey withdrawal rights. For example, an annual premium of $60,000 can be parsed out in $14,000 tax-free gifts to four beneficiaries, leaving a taxable $4,000 amount. With five beneficiaries receiving withdrawal notices, none of the premium transfer to the ILIT would be taxable.

To change the example slightly, if a single trustor has four adult children who will be the beneficiaries of her ILIT, she can give $14,000 to each of them in a year in property, money, or in withdrawal powers from her ILIT. That's $56,000 total tax exclusion gifting. Note that if she gives them other assets outside the ILIT, totaling her annual exclusion amounts she cannot give them tax-free withdrawal rights, too, as the withdrawal rights cannot be in addition to other excluded gifts. But, her annual life insurance premium is only $20,000 per year, leaving her with $36,000 of other, non-ILIT gifts which she can make to those four children. If she divides the $20,000 trust contribution which the trust says she needs to make equally, then she will direct the trustee to notify each child of his right to withdraw $5,000 of cash from the ILIT. That leaves $9,000 of other tax-exclusion gifting which she can make to each child in that year.

Note, however, that there is nothing in the Crummey case language itself nor in any Code or Regulations section which requires that the withdrawal rights be equal among the beneficiaries. The trust language could specify equality, but that would limit the flexibility which could be useful over a long trust period. If, on the other hand, the trust language specifically states that the withdrawal rights designated by the donor do not have to be equally passed out to the beneficiaries, then the trustor in directions made to the trustee can pick and choose which beneficiaries are given the withdrawal rights. In our example above, if mom has already made some large gifts equaling her annual exclusion to child

#1 and child #2, and anticipates child #3 needing some funds near year-end, she could direct the trustee to allocate $14,000 of the $20,000 to child #4 and the remaining $6,000 to child #3. That would still leave $8,000 which Mom could give tax-free to child #3 later in the year.

As the ILIT is irrevocable, there should be some flexibility built into the procedures contained in the documents. Several court cases in the 1990s approved the use of nominal "additional beneficiaries" of the ILIT.[3] By including additional beneficiaries, these beneficiaries expand the gifting opportunities. This is aggressive planning because the IRS fought the use of additional beneficiaries for gifting purposes only. The trustor can only make one $14,000 gift per person per year, and as noted, the transfers to the life insurance trust beneficiaries count like any other gift. If the trustor wants or needs to make annual gifts to his children but he has used up all or a portion of the $14,000 amount per child for that year in making these premium payments, then the trustor is not fully utilizing his gifting capacity to avoid estate taxes. In such a situation, by including additional beneficiaries in the trust, he can, instead, make a premium payment gift to the trust on behalf of one or more of the additional beneficiaries. Within the trust agreement, provisions should be included for naming additional beneficiaries in order to expand the gifting opportunities. Or, perhaps the annual life insurance premium is greater than the gift tax exclusion amount times the number of natural beneficiaries available to a particular trustor.

Bertha's Story. Bertha had only one adult daughter and one adult grandchild to whom she frequently made gifts or forgave short-term loans (which became gifts upon the forgiveness). Her life insurance premium, due to her age was $100,000 per year, so she needed to transfer that much to her ILIT trustee each year, and she was quite averse to the payment

3 *Estate of Christofani v. CIR*, 97 TC 74 (1991) *et seq.*

of any taxes. She had ten friends, however, whom she trusted, and she named each of them in the document as additional beneficiaries. Each year, on her instructions, Bertha's trustee sent letters to those additional beneficiaries, and not to her daughter and granddaughter, giving the friends withdrawal rights. Each year, her attorney prepared gift tax returns for her transfers to the trust to allocate her generation-skipping transfer tax exemption to the trust gifts. The gifts to the additional beneficiaries were never challenged.

The IRS objected unsuccessfully to the Tax Court decisions in the various cases approving the additional beneficiaries, on the ground that those people were not "real" beneficiaries of the trust. As few attorneys want their clients' matters to be the subject of litigation with the IRS, to overcome any IRS objection, it is wise to include provisions in the document to distribute something from the trust to those non-family, non-lineal descendant additional beneficiaries who have received one or more Crummey withdrawal notices from the trustee over the years. Often the ILIT language will include a provision allowing for a breather period of one year after the death of the insured before final distributions are made. In that period, beneficiaries can still receive distributions as needed for health, education, maintenance, and support, and that period allows time for estate issues to get settled. Then the trust can distribute some relatively nominal funds to the additional beneficiaries in order to qualify them as annual gift notice recipients. This provision in the trust should enable the use of additional beneficiaries to withstand IRS scrutiny. If an additional beneficiary never receives a notice, then there should be no obligation on the part of the trustee to make a distribution to that person. In Bertha's Story above, at Bertha's death, her ILIT trustee distributed $50,000 among the surviving additional beneficiaries, as the trust had provided.

10 GUARDIANSHIPS AND CONSERVATORSHIPS

In Chapter 5 about powers of attorney, several documents were recommended in order to avoid certain court processes such as a guardianship and a conservatorship. For those readers unfamiliar with these concepts, having those preventive documents in place may not seem so necessary, urgent, or of dire importance. Additional explanations may be helpful in understanding how critical they can be.

A guardianship and a conservatorship are set up either for a minor or for an adult who is no longer capable of managing his own affairs. While some states use the term guardianship for both, most states distinguish between a guardianship, which is set up to name someone to look after the person (or body) of the minor or incapacitated adult, and a conservatorship, which is established to name someone to look after the assets of the minor or incapacitated adult. While the process can be separated and just a guardianship or just a conservatorship established, often a minor or an incapacitated adult will need both types of fiduciary assistance. Separate people may be appointed for each type of fiduciary needed or one person may serve as both, and co-fiduciaries may also be appointed.

The typical procedure for appointment of a guardian for an incapacitated adult is for an interested party to file a petition in the appropriate court in the state of the residency of the incapacitated adult. Many states handle such matters in the Probate Division of the county court system, but each state determines which of its courts will handle this type of proceeding. The petition must set forth that the adult lacks capacity to maintain himself and to make medical and care decisions. Whether it is at the time of the petition or later in the process, a doctor's statement as to incapacity must be provided to the court and to the alleged incapacitated person. Because due process rights are involved, personal service of legal process on the alleged incapacitated person is normally required, and in most states, the alleged incapacitated person is entitled to have an attorney appointed to represent him during the proceedings. Some courts will also utilize the services of a social worker to make findings or a guardian ad litem for the alleged incapacitated person. The alleged incapacitated person can litigate against the finding of incapacity or the appointment of a particular person as guardian, but it is a difficult process. Ultimately it is the incapacitated person's funds that are used to pay for the guardianship proceedings including professional fees. Depending on state law provisions, a person who is found to be incapacitated is no longer eligible to vote or make his own decisions concerning care, medical treatment, place of residency, etc. If no one is available to be appointed as his guardian, then he may become a ward of the state through the state's or county's public fiduciary office.

Some states now have the concept of limited guardianship for adult guardianships,[1] which is a grant to the guardian of only those powers required by the ward's limitations. The ward is encouraged to be participatory in decisions, to act on his own behalf, and to retain capacity to handle his personal affairs. The idea is to instill maximum self-reliance and independence. In an effort to be sure the ward is completely protected, courts are often reluctant to put limits on the guardian's authority.

The process for appointment of a conservator is similar to that of guardianship. There must be a finding of incapacity. The conservator manages the financial affairs of the protected person. Often a bond is required for the conservator, to give further protection for the ward's assets. Or, the assets can be restricted, requiring court approval for spending. A conservator and a guardian can be paid for their efforts, but the court usually must approve the compensation. Neither conservator or guardian is required to use his own money or other resources for the protected person and can be reimbursed for any such expenditure by the conservatorship estate. Costs and professional fees are paid by the conservator out of the protected person's assets, as well.

The process for appointment of a guardian and a conservator for a minor is similar to that of an adult, except that a finding of minority (under age 18) is all that is needed to support the incapacity aspect.

Who can be a guardian or conservator? A natural or adoptive parent is the natural guardian of a minor. In any kind of guardianship procedure for a minor, one or both parents will prevail over any other party in being appointed guardian, unless they are themselves incapacitated or their parental rights have been previously terminated through

---

1 *See*, for example, Alaska Stat. Sec. 13.26.150(a); Ariz. Rev. Stat. Sec. 14-5312(A)(7); California Prob. Code Sec. 23.51.5; and Ga. Code Ann. Sec. 29-4-22(a) to name a few.

a juvenile dependency proceeding.[2] Parents can name guardians in their Wills for their minor children so that if the parents are deceased or otherwise unable to serve, such other persons are given priority by the court for appointment as guardian.

This naming of guardians for minors is a very important feature of one's Will. It is advisable to name back-up persons, in case the first named person cannot serve. Care should be taken in naming a husband and wife. So, do you really want Uncle Bob serving or is it actually Aunt Irene, the blood relative, who should be the guardian? The Will language can specify that the guardians will be Uncle Bob and Aunt Irene, but if Aunt Irene is or becomes unable to serve, then it can be stated that the guardianship will change to Aunt Susan. Often people will name a relative or friend who is great with people and children to be a guardian. Divorce between guardians also needs to be considered and some statement made as to which one of the divorcing couple should continue as guardian. Other relatives, related by consanguinity or blood relationships, such as grandparents, brothers and sisters, aunts and uncles, etc., are usually given priority by state law, when there is no guardian named in a parent's Will or when no one is otherwise able to serve.

An adult can also name her own guardian, usually in a durable power of attorney or health care power of attorney. It is hoped that by having such documents in place a guardianship can be avoided, but there are circumstances in which a guardianship may become necessary in spite of the documentation. In order to exercise one's free will, it is important to have personal guardian provisions in your documents.

The conservator is a fiduciary with a high duty of

2 Juvenile dependency proceedings are beyond the scope of this book. Dependency proceedings are often brought by the state in abuse or neglect cases, but many states have procedures for private parties to bring such actions.

responsibility and care to oversee money and property for the benefit of the ward or protected person, and to properly invest funds for income and growth and to look after real estate and other property which may be part of the conservatorship estate. The conservator can be any adult the court finds to be a proper party. Most states have priority lists, including first, a parent, then whomever a deceased parent might name in his Will, and then persons closely associated to the minor or incapacitated adult by consanguinity, or blood relations. A conservator should be someone who is rational and either good with finances or who has sufficient sophistication to hire advisors for assistance. Parents of minor children will sometimes name a different person as conservator rather than empower a guardian with monetary responsibilities as well as the personal care job. Most states' courts have set strict standards for how conservatorship funds can be invested and require annual or more frequent accountings for how funds are spent. They often require court approval for all expenditures except daily living expenses of the protected person, and impose a bond on the conservator, so there is insurance in the event the conservator commits malfeasance. Money is a big tempter, and even the best people are drawn into bad actions when readily accessible money is at hand. It is against the law for a conservator to use the Ward's money for personal purposes, even loans. A conservator can pay himself for his work, but the best course of action is to ask the court to approve a specific payment for conservator fees. The court has the power to force the conservator to pay back excessive or unapproved fees and expenditures, belonging to the incapacitated person, to use the funds solely

The concept behind a conservatorship for a minor is that the legal rights of minors are limited. Minors cannot, for instance, own property in their own names. Conservatorships for minors often arise in accident claim situations. If your minor son is involved in a bicycle accident in which he is injured from being hit by a car, the car driver, if found to be responsible for causing the accident, will be liable for damages, including medical costs and pain and suffering connected with the injuries. If your child receives either a judgment against the driver or a settlement amount, those funds belong to him. In order to claim the funds, you as the parent must petition to the court to be appointed as his conservator to hold the funds. Even though you are the natural guardian of your son, the court must find that you are an appropriately behaving person in order to appoint you as conservator. You will be directed to put the funds into special investments, often restricted as to use. You cannot use your son's own money for his care and support to the extent that you have a parental obligation to support your son. You can petition the court to use the funds for other purposes, in excess of the parental obligation of support, and the court will consider your petition, your son's situation, and the requested use of the funds. When your son reaches age 18, unless he is otherwise incapacitated, the conservatorship ends, and you will be required to turn over ownership of the funds to him, now that he is legally an adult. Proper guidance and teaching about the importance of money should be incorporated into the education you give your son, so that upon receiving the funds which have been carefully held for his benefit in the conservatorship, he does not unwisely use the money and quickly dissipate the funds.

Since a minor cannot own property in her own right, several decades ago the National Conference of Commissioners on Uniform State Laws proposed and drafted a set of statutes called the Uniform Gifts to Minors Act ("UGMA" for short), which was adopted in a variety of forms by the various states. In the 1980s, the Uniform Transfers to Minors Act ("UTMA") was proposed and adopted by many states as a replacement to UGMA. The idea behind both Acts was the same, and the provisions are based on legislation enacted in each state. A set of rules exists for holding the minor's property in a special account, an UTMA or UGMA account, controlled by a custodian, for the minor's benefit. State law varies as to when the donee may remove the property from the account: age 18, 21, 24, etc. Transfer to an UTMA account for a minor is a completed gift, which means that the donor may no longer utilize the property or funds for his own usage, but rather the property is now part of the minor's assets. The custodian may make the determination to alter the investment of the asset or even to use it for the minor's benefit, but the asset may not be used to satisfy any parental obligation of support. The custodian has a fiduciary duty to the minor to invest and use the fund wisely.

There is no limit on what can be put in an UTMA/UGMA account: cash in banks, stock and securities in brokerage accounts, limited partnership interests, deeds to real estate, and so forth. A transfer to a minor such as this is a taxable gift unless the gift qualifies for the gift tax annual exclusion. Unlike a gift to a trust, which is more difficult to qualify for the annual exclusion, the UTMA gift is assumed to be a gift of a present interest, so UTMA gifts are common for fairly small amounts of gifts and accumulations of earnings, when the donor does not fear too much misuse of the assets in the hands of a young adult.

Gifting Grandmother Story. Grandmother wanted to give her 5 grandchildren some money each year, but she did not want their parents to have access to the funds for fear that they'd squander it. She asked her banker, who helped her set up 5 UTMA accounts, and Grandmother named her younger brother, the grandchildren's great uncle Jonah, as the custodian of each account. The banker told her that under the laws of that state, each grandchild could claim ownership of his or her account at age 21. Each year, as she could, Grandmother made transfers to the accounts. When the sixth grandchild came along, she made larger gifts to that grandchild's UTMA account for a while until he was equalized with the others. As the accounts grew in value, Uncle Jonah invested the funds in mutual funds and government bonds. Grandmother did not tell her children or grandchildren what she was doing. At age 21, each grandchild got a big surprise of a distribution of several thousand dollars which had been growing and being added to by their grandmother for more than a decade. While other mechanisms could have been utilized, such as trusts, the UTMA accounts were an easy and inexpensive way for Grandmother to recognize her grandchildren and give them meaningful gifts.

11 MINOR'S TRUST

Parents, grandparents, aunts, uncles, godparents and others who may wish to leave assets at death to a minor child (someone under age 18) or is interested in giving one or more large gifts during life should consider utilizing a trust to hold the assets. Such a trust can be set up as a stand-alone document, in a Will, or as part of a revocable living trust. It is very important to provide trusts for minor children and young adult children. As discussed in Chapter 10, a gift outright or award or other transfer of assets to a child under age 18 requires, in most jurisdictions, the establishment of a court-ordered conservatorship. Children under age 18 are considered "disabled" under the law as a result of their minority age. From an estate planning perspective, a parent naming a minor child directly as a beneficiary or contingent beneficiary of a retirement plan or life insurance policy will ensure one or both of the following unappealing consequences will happen:

- a conservatorship must be established to own the assets for the child until she reaches age 18 (*see* discussion in Chapter 10 regarding conservatorship); or

- the child will receive his inheritance either at age 18 when the conservatorship ends or a young adult will receive a sum of money or other item of property perhaps at a time when he is not emotionally mature enough to handle it or lacks other resources to support property ownership.

It is useful to think about the size of your estate and the number of children who will be inheriting from you, when considering whether to have a trust for children placed in your Will or living trust document. If you have 3 minor children, a house, car, savings account, 401(k) plan through work, and life insurance policy through work, you could easily have a $300,000 to $400,000 estate. If your estate is distributed outright to your children at your death, could each of them responsibly handle $100,000 of inheritance at age 18? Would they have the ability to cooperate with each other to pool their cash to maintain the home until it could be sold? Can they agree among themselves about how to manage and split the assets? Would they know to consult legal counsel, an accountant, and/or a financial advisor for help with the assets, entering into written agreements among themselves, tax planning decisions, and making wise investment choices? Or, would the house fall into disrepair, the funds used instead for games, cars, clothes, etc., and essentially be squandered? Given the lack of financial literacy of younger people today in this country, it is more likely that the latter scenario will occur. Children are not necessarily "bad," but rather they lack the skills and maturity needed for careful money management. An old estate planner's joke asks the question, "How long does take an 18 year old to go through an inheritance?" The answer is twenty minutes! The truth is not that much different than the joke.

The alternative to outright distribution is to set up within your Will or your revocable living trust agreement, a trust for minor and young adult children. You would name one or more people as trustee or co-trustees over the trust, and the trustee will be required by law to administer the trust for your children according to the terms of the trust. The trust can provide that funds are to be expended for your children's health, education, maintenance and support (known as the "HEMS" standard) while they are minors and into their adulthood. The assets in the trust will be distributed outright to the children only when the trust provides, so you can choose to have your children's inheritances held until they reach certain life milestones such as college graduation or beyond or reach certain ages. The larger the inheritance, the longer a trust needs to be held for the beneficiary rather than be distributed. While the funds are in trust, the child's creditors cannot make claims against those funds, because the assets are owned by the trust and not by the child. Anti-creditor provisions in a trust are referred to as "spend thrift" provisions because they prevent the beneficiary from wasting the trust principal. More importantly, the use of the trust prevents a child's creditors or other claimants from taking the inheritance.

Another reason to use a trust in your Will is if you have a child with "special needs." This reference is to disabilities which may prevent your child from living an ordinary life and which may cause her to require special treatment. If your special needs child qualifies for any kind of governmental assistance, which is often based on financial resources ("needs based"), leaving an inheritance outright to such a child will make her ineligible for such government assistance, until the funds are spent down or are contributed to a different kind of trust, requiring court approval. It is important to caution relatives, such as grandparents, to adjust their own estate planning documents to take your child's special needs into consideration. Providing a discretionary trust for the challenged child or adult in which the trustee makes decisions about distributions and use of funds for the benefit of the child or adult, can maintain the child's ability to receive government funding plus provide a means to pay for extras.

12 HOW A BENEFICIARY "BENEFITS" FROM YOUR TRUST

If you have not read a trust lately, or ever, you may not be familiar with some fairly standard provisions contained in the agreement regarding how the trust provides benefits for named beneficiaries. Those beneficiaries could be your spouse, children, grandchildren, other relatives or friends, and charities.

First, let's look at how you identify your beneficiaries. If you do not have children, then you may be leaving your estate to charities or to other relatives such as siblings, nieces and nephews, cousins, etc. If you have children, then the usual course is to name your children and present or future grandchildren as beneficiaries. A commonly used term in Wills and trusts is <u>issue</u> which is a simple way to describe your lineal descendants, that is, your children, grandchildren, great grandchildren, and so on. It might be used as follows: "I give the remainder of my estate in equal shares to my two children or to their issue."

It is also important to specify how the estate is to be distributed if you have issue who predecease you. In the example above, you have left your estate on a per capita basis to your children, one share "per head" or per person.

If your son has one child and your daughter has three children, how do you want to leave your estate if one child predeceases you? You could say, "or to the survivor thereof," which means that only your surviving child would receive the entire estate. Or you could provide a *per stirpes* distribution which would always provide for a two-way split of your estate, one-half going to the son's child and one-half being split three ways among your daughter's children. The third way would be to say "by right of representation," which will be the same as a *per stirpes* distribution if only one child predeceases you. If both children predecease you, however, it would provide for an equal division among all four of your grandchildren, treating each one at that level of consanguinity as equal beneficiaries.

The following is some standard income and principal language for a trust income beneficiary.

a. Distribution of Net Income. The trustee shall pay to the beneficiary, or apply for his or her benefit, the entire net income of the beneficiary's trust in annual or more frequent installments as the beneficiary may direct.

b. Distribution of Funds for Necessities. In addition, if at any time in the discretion of the trustee the beneficiary should be in need of funds for his or her proper health, education, maintenance and support, the trustee shall pay to him or her, or apply for his or her benefit, such sums from the principal of the beneficiary's trust as the trustee deems necessary or advisable for such purposes. In making any payments of principal to or for the benefit of the beneficiary under this paragraph, the trustee shall take into consideration, to the extent the trustee deems advisable, any other resources of the beneficiary, outside this trust, known to the trustee.

There are administrative issues to be considered in writing and administering a trust agreement. Factors we need to think about in how our trusts are to provide benefits to the beneficiaries include changes in the nature of wealth, financial instruments, how income is produced (capital gains, interest, or dividends), marketability of property, the fact that our trusts are generally lasting for decades, the need for increasing flexibility in dealing with beneficiaries, and a recognition that in the future, trusts may have different tax treatment.

In addition, inherent conflict between the needs of the income beneficiary and remainder beneficiary must be addressed. As an example of each, your trust may provide for your children during their lifetimes with the trust funds to be distributed to your grandchildren at the children's deaths. What works well for an investment strategy for one does not always work for the other. Corporate trustees often talk about serving two masters, the current beneficiaries and those whose rights mature later. The trustee's challenge is to find investments which will provide income as well as growth to the fund to meet the needs of those two masters.

Two alternatives, the unitrust approach and the annuity approach, may eliminate these administrative and investment quandaries of balancing the needs of the current beneficiaries and the future beneficiaries. Called by a variety of titles, "total return investing," the "all income" trust, etc., the concept seeks to provide a means to give the trustee power to invest in a "total return" rather than being driven to generate a certain amount of "income" as that term is traditionally defined.[1] By structuring the trust as a

1 *See* Glossary, Chapter 33.

unitrust or an annuity trust, the trustee has a framework on which to operate and beneficiaries' expectations can be defined, as opposed to just giving broad powers to the trustee which may lead to misunderstandings and poor planning. For example, bonds may be paying low interest rates (an income component) while stocks are appreciating in value (a principal component). With a total return investing approach, the trustee can make more generous distributions to the income beneficiaries, while seeking growth for the ultimate advantage of the remainder beneficiaries.

The following is sample language for a total return trust:

> In each taxable year of the trust, the trustee shall pay to the beneficiary during the beneficiary's lifetime, a unitrust amount (hereinafter the "unitrust amount") equal to a fixed percentage (hereinafter the "fixed percentage") of five percent (5%) of the net fair market value of the trust assets valued as of the close of the last business day of the preceding tax year of the trust (hereinafter "valuation date"). Any income of the trust for a taxable year in excess of the unitrust amount shall be added to principal.

There are some difficulties with using the total return concept so it may not work in all situations. Non-marketable assets are expensive to value each year, but the document can give the trustee discretion concerning the valuation. The income beneficiary's need for principal can be satisfied by giving the trustee emergency discretion to invade principal (which would reduce possibly the unitrust amount received in subsequent years). The burden of low investment yields will be shouldered as much by the remainder beneficiary as by the income beneficiary, but trust language should focus the trustee's concerns for the income beneficiary's needs, as planners typically try to do with the income-principal approach. If income is greater than the unitrust amount would yield, then the trustee could be given discretion to pay out the greater of the unitrust amount or income. Qualification of a trust for QTIP treatment to obtain the marital deduction for estate or gift tax purposes requires that all income be distributed to the surviving spouse. A provision should be included to allow the trustee to distribute an amount equal to the greater of trust net income for the year or the unitrust amount.

Certain trusts may not be suited for the unitrust approach. Credit shelter or bypass trusts should not necessarily be structured as total return trusts because the value of sheltering the corpus from estate taxes on the principal portion distributed will be lost. A generation-skipping trust where nonskip persons are included does not work well because a portion of the funds would be subject to estate tax earlier than necessary. Spendthrift trusts should be carefully considered before conversion because the total return trust will open more trust principal to the reach of a beneficiary's creditors. Finally, trusts of nonliquid assets could require distribution in-kind or forced sales of assets.

It is important to choose the proper percentage to pay out for the total return. Most financial studies indicate that over the long haul, a percentage of 3% to 5% will preserve the fund for continuation. The amount can be adjusted for inflation, or the percentage can be based on an average of three years of trust valuation. In looking at the unitrust model, most of the time there will be a significant change at about 15-16 years, so a low percentage works well with a long-term trust.

The annuity approach provides a fixed percentage payable each year to the beneficiaries based on an initial valuation of the assets. Annuity language can read as follows:

> In each taxable year of the trust, the trustee shall pay to the beneficiary an annuity amount equal to five percent (5%) of the net fair market value of the assets of the trust valued as of the date of the initial funding of the trust.

One difficulty in dealing with the annuity approach is that if there is a decline in the value of assets, the annuity approach will maintain income stability for the income beneficiary but will erode the principal amount. Conversely, the income beneficiary will not participate in any subsequent appreciation in value of the trust estate. The annuity amount could be indexed for inflation, if there is concern that the growth of the principal will be disadvantageous to the income beneficiary.

13 LEAVING A LEGACY AND SENDING THE CORRECT MESSAGE ABOUT MONEY TO YOUR HEIRS

Life, as we know, is short, even for the long-lived among us. Most of us at some time during our lives have wanted to be noted, remembered, and appreciated for some of the things we have done. Leaving a valuable legacy is something each of us can do. For some, making parts of their legacy is a daily goal. The endeavor does not have to be massive, like getting your name put on a building, and it can be simple to implement. First, you have to have something of value to impart. If you are already doing that in your present life whether it's raising children or volunteering for charity, you are making a legacy. If your legacy concerns money, you may wish to pay special attention to how you frame your communications to your heirs.

Money and wealth created by having money are complicated topics which can spawn many psychological variants. Conveying the correct message about money should be a key goal in your estate planning. By its nature, an inheritance, whether large or small, is someone else's money bestowed upon the recipient beneficiary. The beneficiary for the most part has done nothing to earn the money himself. Parents who have worked hard to support the family during their working years and are able to leave an inheritance to their children are giving their money to the children. Most parents are anxious to leave an inheritance to their children and grandchildren. Usually the children and grandchildren are happy to receive the inheritance, but there may not be a correct appreciation level there. It has taken hard work for the parents to have it to leave, and it is easy for the children to be the recipients. Unless there are psychological games being played or unpaid care-giving, the children may have paid nothing for the inheritance. Your documents, therefore, need to help you send the correct message to your children about the money and other property, what it means to you, and what it can do for them. And, that message is an augmentation of the financial part of your legacy.

What can you do? The legal documents are rather fixed in that certain provisions must be included, but there is opportunity to add special language about your life and legacy. Customize your trust so that the messages you wish to be sent are clear. Tell your attorney that you want your special language added. In addition to provisions in your Will or trust, you can leave letters and instructions for things that you want. Share the concepts with your legal counsel, however, to be sure that the format you choose will be enforceable and frankly, to test the reasonableness of your messages. Burial wishes, funeral plans, suggestions to guardians of your minor children, treatment of employees and other important people in your life, lists of beneficiaries of personal effects that are important to you, statements of love and worth – these are all ways that you can be sure others understand your values, your wishes, your life lessons, and other pieces which go into making your legacy. These are significant messages, no matter the size of your estate.

One clear way to communicate the importance of the inheritance is to protect it. By leaving children's and grandchildren's shares in trust, with appropriate distribution provisions, their use of the funds is 1) controlled and 2) protected. Income from interest, dividends, rents, and royalties can be distributed to the beneficiaries, but the amount of income produced can often be controlled by the investments made with trust funds. Principal (which includes capital gains) can be held back and distributed for specific purposes. Health, education, maintenance and support is the general standard, but pure discretionary distributions can and should be authorized. Guidance can be given to the trustee for discretionary distributions such as allowances for a first house or a down payment, investing in a business, wedding expenses, etc. Trust funds can also be used to invest in items which benefit the beneficiary without him actually owning the assets: the trust can own a house, business investments, vacation property, etc., all of which the beneficiary can utilize. And, there are other formulas for distribution such as the total return of percentage of value each year[1] or by matching distributions to a beneficiary's earnings, perhaps with exceptions for responsible, low-paying, socially beneficial jobs (teachers, nonprofits, social workers, etc.).

Anything left in trust for the beneficiary and not distributed out to him is protected from creditor claims. This is an extra, very special gift to the beneficiary. What you have left to the beneficiary in trust is not subject to divorce, judgments (think about judgments against a spouse for which your child might be responsible), and even bankruptcy, so long as the beneficiary has no ownership or ability alone to control the trust's assets. Your legacy is protected in this way.

Trusts can now be held for many generations, depending on state law. Trusts can last "in perpetuity" or for a very long

1 *See* discussion in Chapter 12.

term.[2] Thus you can extend the protections afforded by the trust for many generations. It is hoped that as time goes by, the beneficiaries will learn the value of having the financial protection of a trust fund, which if the fund were given outright, may have been here today and very much gone (read, squandered) tomorrow.

There are other benefits to leaving the trust in place for multiple generations. Conservatively invested with reasonable distributions for income, taxes, and principal distributions, the trust fund can grow significantly through the years. That leaves a very valuable legacy of your wealth and builds an appreciation of money for many generations.

Further, you can customize your trust to include a philanthropic component. Trusts set up by the Rockefeller families, now having benefited many generations, require each beneficiary to adopt a philanthropic aim, to use a portion of trust funds in advancing that project, etc. You can follow that model and direct that there be annual meetings of beneficiaries to report on the use of funds; designations by beneficiaries of charities to receive part of the trust at a beneficiary's death; and make it a condition that a beneficiary do good works before she receives any funds.[3]

A mission statement in your trust for your heirs can be meaningful. It can explain the family's or your individual philosophy about wealth, how the wealth was obtained, what sacrifices were made to get the wealth or to keep it, the meaning of charity and charitable giving to the family, and what recipient heirs should do in their lives to preserve the wealth or make it serve its valuable purpose. By setting forth your directives, you can make a difference in how your family views the wealth you have generously left to them.

---

2 *See* Arizona Revised Statutes Sec. 14-2901 which authorizes a 500 year trust term limitation.
3 The movie, The Ultimate Gift, portrays this message very effectively.

Roger's and Susan's Story. Roger and Susan live a comfortable lifestyle, and they have three successful, educated adult daughters. Roger and Susan never wanted their middle class affluence to ruin their children's motivations. When they set up their revocable living trust, they asked that it benefit multiple generations. Then they requested a condition be imposed on the trustees and beneficiaries. Each year, the beneficiaries are required to write a report to the trustees about how they are doing, what they are doing significantly in their work and lives, and what their charitable activities have consisted of. They also are required to have an annual meeting, paid for by the trust, to get together, to know each other, and to share their ideas about life and helping others.

Even if you are leaving a good deal of money to your children, the way Roger and Susan are, you can strengthen the financial legacy you are leaving by providing guidance and teaching to your heirs about the value of money, the true value of the inheritance, the amount of effort it took to get it and keep it, the due diligence needed to look out for it so it is not wasted or lost, a meaningful purpose to be done with it, etc. Your job is to inspire and motivate, and if your heir or heirs are just not "getting it," then perhaps your financial legacy should be seriously tied to requirements and restrictions. What may not be perceived well today by those heirs, may one day provide the basis for their good acts, if you preserve the wealth in trust. Maturity can take a long time to come to certain people.

Rita's Story. Living a good, noble life is one of the finest things a person can do. Rita has been deceased for 20 years, but those who knew her remember her for her daily kindnesses, and for her constant motto, "Be good to each other." That legacy has been far more valuable to her children, spouse, and friends than any money she left behind.

14 HANDLING THE DETAILS OF LIFE

There are an amazing number of important things that fill our daily lives in this 21st century. When a person's life ends or when incapacity limits a person's control over life, other people must step in to handle all the myriad details of that deceased or incapacitated person's life – details that he may not have thought to clarify for the benefit of others. Those helpers need to be able to stand in the shoes of the deceased or incapacitated, find out what is pending, figure out what needs to be done right now, and take responsibility for future steps. Too often it's a process of sleuthing at its most difficult. But it need not be.

This discussion is for you, the living and competent, to assist you in identifying those actions you should consider taking RIGHT NOW to create a usable record of your life so that others can immediately pick up where you have left off, either for your own care or for the benefit of your heirs.[1] But it is also important for you to be organized, know where your information is, and keep track of your affairs. It may take some extra time in the beginning, but it will save you time and trouble going forward. Chances are, you will make better decisions, because you will have easier and greater access to your personal data.

This outline is organized into various headings representative of some of the larger categories of our life activities. They are not discreet categories, and the outline is not meant to be all inclusive. As you consider it, you will undoubtedly think of many other "must do" items. Its purpose is to serve as a guide or checklist to help you put a structure in place to make later detective work by others into your affairs more fruitful. This list of things to do represents the wisdom accumulated from countless estate situations where friends or family have been faced with stepping into someone else's shoes.

Mary's Story. Not surprisingly, the key is to keep careful records, logically organized. When Mary died at a young and vibrant age of cancer, she had done some quick preparation in having estate planning documents put in place, but no one took the time to look closely at her beautiful home to discover the wreck it was with respect to her personal papers. She had been a very successful business person, was educated, and yes, should have known better. But, her bank statements were randomly stuffed in kitchen drawers with the silverware; organizer boxes and packets of file folders were still unwrapped in the top of her closet; and her desk drawers were crammed with stubby pencils, horse hoof picks, and a smattering of significant papers like her birth certificate. Putting her financial estate together took the corporate trustee many hours and lots of extra fees charged to the estate and resulted in delayed distributions to the beneficiaries.

---

1 Please note that this list of items is by no means exhaustive.

Personal and Financial Matters

Paperwork. Over the years as we have helped settle estates, we have found that the less organized estates demand a careful search of every inch of one's quarters, generates a lot of trash, and wastes time and money. It is recommended that you get yourself and your documents organized as follows:

- Have ready access to a filing cabinet with plenty of storage space.

- Use clearly labeled file folders with plain text headings. Consider an indexing system even if it's just an alphabetical list of the file folders.

- Be security conscious. Consider a safe deposit box, locking or fireproof cabinet or safe, at home or at a secure location. Be sure to keep track of the key and/ or combination and let only trusted other people know about it.

- Consider making duplicate copies of critically important documents, kept at a separate location.

- Any document with personally identifiable information should be shredded when discarded. The best rule is to never put anything personally identifiable in your garbage or recyclable containers. Anyone who handles your personal or financial affairs should observe the same rule. Use a shredder which cross-cut and really grinds the pages. Straight shredders leave strips of paper which methamphetamine addicts or even children with patience can tape together to retrieve your personal data.

- Discard or scan out-of-date paperwork/statements. The general rule is keep tax-related items for seven years and other statements for five years. After that, shred it! Mark statements as "closed," "sold," or "transferred" for accounts that are no longer in existence. It is often extremely confusing for people administering estates to determine what assets or accounts are still in existence.

Credit Reports

- Everyone is entitled to a free credit report from each agency each year. If you stagger your free reports (*e.g.*, request Equifax in January, TransUnion in May, and Experian in September) you can do a decent job of monitoring your credit reports for free every few months.

- If you are concerned that the security of your identity or credit is at risk, monitoring services such as Lifelock (which is not specifically endorsed here) can be purchased for a small monthly fee.

- Any problem you find on one credit report should be reported to all of the credit agencies -- all of the credit agencies should respond with a copy of the report showing that the item is not listed on their report or that the matter is under investigation (this is another way to get an "extra" free copy of your credit report).

- If you suspect that you have been a victim of identity theft, you can generally get your credit report for free, even if you have used your free annual report already that year.

- You can also request a copy of your CLUE and A PLUS report which show insurance history (accidents, claims etc.) and can affect insurance rates, credit, etc.

- Credit reporting agencies, including Choicepoint (the major issuer of CLUE reports) sell your information to people who might be interested in selling you insurance, offering you credit, etc. By opting out (*i.e.,* requesting that your information not be sold in this manner), you reduce the risk of something being sent to you in the mail being stolen and used to steal your identity. By permanently opting out (which must be done in writing), your FICO credit score may even jump by a few points.

Accounts at Banks, Brokerages, and Other Investment Locations

- Keep account statements organized.

- Keep a list of your accounts and update the list regularly.

- Consider consolidating multiple accounts.

- Keep in mind FDIC limits for protection of your bank accounts.

- Adding another person to an account (or other asset) as a co-owner for convenience purposes can have unintended legal consequences. Don't do it. Issue that person a power of attorney instead, so they can sign as your fiduciary and not as a joint owner.

Computer

- Computer Systems. Most of what we do is still subject to a paper record, especially in the legal realm. So, even if you've gone substantially "paperless" and organized your life with the help of sophisticated computer programs, you still need a logical system of organization.

- Scanning. Physical records can be scanned for storage and then filed away or, in appropriate circumstances, shredded. Of course, all original signed documents need to be kept intact. One virtue of scanning is unlimited economical storage space, leading to the maxim, "When in doubt, save it, scan it." Ideally, you will have organized your scanned records for easy access.

Online Accounts

- Computers crash. Set up automatic back-up systems. And, if there is any possibility of a significant consequence in the future if a document is no longer available, consider making a physical copy.

- Computer programs and systems change. Whenever you update your computer system, be sure that all of your existing files are compatible with the new system and can still be accessed without difficulty.

- Keep a physical list of accounts you access on the internet.

- Keep your passwords in writing and stored somewhere safe and secure but accessible.

- For identity theft purposes, vary your passwords and avoid birth dates and obvious words and names identifiable as yours. One excellent rule of thumb is to use passwords having at least eight (8) characters, including both upper and lower case alpha characters, numbers and grammatical marks.

- Change your online passwords periodically. One method is to adopt an annual or bi-annual date on which you update your passwords such as on your birthday, tax day, or anniversary. Calendar the date to remind you to take this important step.

Computer Security

- If you are using Microsoft Windows, updates, including

security updates, are issued several times per month. Your computer should notify you that updates are available. Make sure you are running these updates regularly. Other operating systems offer similar services.

- You should have quality virus scan software installed on your computer. Virus scan software also must be updated regularly through downloads issued by the provider.

Real Estate

- Keep deeds or copies of deeds in your records. Consider keeping a duplicate copy in a separate file or location. Some deeds are readily available online, but not all states and countries have updated their recording systems. The same is true for the Abstract to your property, if your real estate is located in an Abstract state.

- Review your deeds from time to time to be sure the ownership is reflected correctly and in the best way.

- Remove names of deceased or divorced co-owners from deeds. Your lawyer or a title company can assist you with this process.

- When property is owned by multiple persons who are not spouses, consider using a partnership or limited liability company format for ownership, instead of placing multiple names on the deed.

Other Assets

- Keep a list or index of other assets and title paperwork.

- Regularly update all documents, accounts, titles and other listings when there have been deaths, divorces, marriages, or births.

Tax Matters

- Keep your tax returns, all of them, even if you store them electronically.

- Keep income statements, receipts for deductible items, bank statements and check registers for 5-7 years.

- Tax returns are one way to help your detective locate your assets.

Personal Effects

- Make a list of beneficiaries for special items.

- Leave a list of instructions regarding your wishes for sale and donation.

- Spend a day with a clipboard or laptop or notebook computer listing your property. The list is often useful to have later.

- Consider taking pictures or a video for insurance purposes in the event of fire or other catastrophe.

Personal Finances

- Write down a "snapshot" of your personal financial system. Where does the money come from and where does it go? What is your accounting system? When do bills come in and how are they paid? Where do you do your banking and what is each account used for?

- If a catastrophe occurs, the bills will keep coming in, and the day-to-day financial decisions will still need to be made. Basically, whom do you entrust with that responsibility?

- Consider the following in the event of your sudden demise or incapacity:

- What should be done in the first twenty-four hours and who should do it?

- What should be done in the first thirty days? Who should do what?

- What should happen after that – in the short term and in the longer term?

- Evaluate whether your life insurance is sufficient. Life insurance can be useful for tax planning, to provide liquidity for your estate, provide asset protection and be a creditor-protected investment, and provide other benefits. Consider and consult with an attorney regarding the estate tax implications of having life insurance. *See* Chapter 9.

- On average, every generation is living longer than the previous generation. Seriously consider purchasing a long-term care insurance policy. Many people who plan to utilize Medicaid as a funding source will not qualify for coverage. They will not meet its strict financial eligibility requirements. If Medicaid is a real possibility, plan at least 5 years in advance of the need for such services in order to transfer and give assets appropriately to meet the financial eligibility requirements. Ideally, this will be part of your overall estate plan. Consult with an elder care attorney to discuss your options. *See* Chapter 31.

Health Care

- Discuss your health issues with your family so that they are not surprised about them later. Even after your death, they may still need the information. Ultimately, you should confide in someone.

- Keep a list of your doctors and medications in a place where family members know to look for them. Update this list frequently. Look over the list on a given day every month or so and calendar the date.

- Take your medication list along when you travel.

- Do not assume that a doctor, clinic, hospital, government agency or other provider will keep your medical records forever. They do not. Each doctor maintains his own records, so it is up to you to make sense of them.

- If possible, regularly get your own copy of medical and lab reports and jot down why you are seeing each doctor and what each doctor has said or recommended. If possible, get copies of your doctors' written reports. Keep all of these records in an organized system. This medical history will be of great help to you or your helper later.

- Spend an afternoon, once or twice a year, reviewing your medical files to make sure they are organized and intelligible.

- If appropriate, include specific family members in your medical appointments and/or records review. If they should become responsible for your care, they will value knowing your doctors and your medical history.

- Have a Health Care Power of Attorney and let your agent know your treatment wishes.

- Have a Living Will and orally let your agent and family know how far you want life sustaining treatment to be continued before it is stopped.

- People often dread thinking about death and incapacity. The first step is to get over this hump. The second is to consult experts to learn your options. The third step is to consult your loved ones and trusted advisors. Make your decisions. Then, have "the talk" with your family.

- Consider whether it is advisable to create a video record of your decisions or the thinking behind those decisions, for use later should there be any question.

- Be careful if appointing a health care agent whose personal beliefs may prevent them from carrying out your health care and end-of-life treatment decisions.

- Provide a copy of your health care power of attorney and living will to your doctors. Take a copy with you for any hospital or clinic treatment.

- If your health care power of attorney or living will is registered with a state agency, a service which is provided in several states, updates must also be registered in order to ensure they are given full legal effect.

- Travel with your documents. You never know when an emergency will strike. Place a copy of critical documents in your wallet or purse or, at minimum, a notice to providers about whom to contact or where to locate your documents. If you travel abroad, investigate the availability of medical care in the locations you will be visiting. Many health care providers in the world will neither understand nor honor powers of attorney or other U.S. legal documents.

- Consider purchasing "air-evac" medical transport insurance, particularly if you will be spending a long time away from home in a foreign locale.

Burial or Cremation

- Discuss your burial or cremation and disposition desires with your family. This is especially important if there is a likelihood that a dispute could occur.

- Have a burial or cremation statement which is both witnessed and notarized, and in it name who is in charge of carrying out your wishes.

- Discuss or write down funeral or memorial service wishes.

- Think about making prepaid arrangements through a funeral home.

Social Security Administration

- If you are receiving social security benefits, keep the record of benefits, phone numbers, bank deposits, etc., in your file cabinet in a labeled folder.

- Your personal representative (*i.e.,* executor) should know to call Social Security once you are deceased.

Estate Planning Documents

- Know where your original documents are and make sure your successor trustee or personal representative knows where your originals are and can easily access them. If they are being held by an attorney with whom you are no longer in contact, consider taking possession of the original documents. If that attorney retires or moves, it will be difficult for your family to locate your originals after your death, adding unnecessary legal costs to the administration of your estate.

- If your originals are held in a safe deposit box, make sure the appropriate people can easily access the box if you are incapacitated or deceased. For instance, if you hold your box in the name of your revocable living trust, your successor trustee should be able to access the box upon a showing of your death or incapacity, the trust, and his credentials.

- Review your documents periodically to ensure that the people who you have named as your agents (trustees, personal representatives, guardians for minor children, health care agents, and attorneys-in-fact) are still able to serve and are still the persons you wish to have serving in those roles. Confirm that your distribution provisions are still appropriate (deceased beneficiaries should be removed or modified, after-born children or grandchildren may need to be set forth if beneficiaries are identified by name rather than as a general class, assets should not be left outright to beneficiaries who cannot handle the money or who are receiving needs-based government insurance or other benefits; etc.).

- Re-execute your powers of attorney every few years even if no changes are needed. Institutions such as banks, brokerage firms, and title companies are often hesitant to accept powers of attorney that are more than a few years old.

- Periodically review beneficiaries on life insurance, retirement assets, etc. Consider the potentially undesirable legal consequences of naming a minor as a beneficiary on such assets.

-Remember that your beneficiary designations on life insurance policies, IRAs, retirement plans, annuities, etc. will override all provisions in your Will, so it is important to coordinate your Will with the beneficiary designations.

-If you have a trust, ensure that ownership of all assets have been transferred to it (by title change, assignment, or other method appropriate to the particular asset) in order to avoid unnecessary court proceedings in the event of death or incapacity. If you refinance real property, it is often standard procedure to remove real estate from a trust as part of the refinancing transaction. Any property that has been removed from a trust for refinancing purposes should be returned to the trust as soon as possible thereafter.

- Authorize your fiduciary in your Will, trust, or power of attorney to obtain access to your online financial accounts, social media sites, etc.

Work or Business

Next in Charge

- Name someone in writing to pick up and be in charge if you cannot be there for a period of time or permanently. Execute a Special Power of Attorney in the event of a planned absence.

- Authorize in writing the hiring of an outside manager to run the business, if that is what is needed.

- Have a written business plan even if it is your solo business.

- Take the time to write down what you do, how you do it and what you would want someone else to do if you were suddenly out of the picture. Be sure to pass along your accumulated business wisdom.

- Have business continuation insurance.

- Have a life insurance policy to pay your family for your share of the business or to replace the income from the business if its operations are impaired or closed.

- If you have co-owners, to avoid misunderstanding, have a "buy-sell" agreement in place with a valuation formula and a payment plan, which should include life insurance, if possible.

Work in Progress

- Keep an on-going list as part of your normal work plan with notes regarding contacts, what comes next, etc., so that the business can continue effectively.

- Professionals such as attorneys, doctors, and therapists should consider having "Professional Living Wills" indicating who is to take over their patient/client files in the event of their own death or incapacity.

Financial Matters

- Be sure someone knows what it takes in terms of income, customers, orders, etc., to keep the business afloat financially.

- Arrange for bill paying, payroll, taxes, etc., to be handled if you are not there. Failure to pay payroll taxes, even in the event of an emergency, can have devastating legal and financial consequences.

Whew! Does all of this sound like way too much detail? Consider how difficult it is to step into another person's shoes with no preparation whatsoever. You would want to do what he would have you do. But, at that moment, he cannot communicate those wishes to you...unless he has taken the time in advance to document the details of his life. Do the same organization for yourself and your helpers.

15 LIFE CYCLE ESTATE PLANNING

As time goes by, our lives change. It is important for each of us to keep our planning and the documents which implement that planning up to date. The following is a discussion of a few of the key estate planning documents that you need to have in place at various times in your life.

Parents of Minor Children

At the very least, parents of minor children should have Wills that name a guardian for the minor children and a conservator for the children's estates. The process for having a guardian approved by the court is often much simpler when there is a Will making the appointment of a guardian than it is when a guardian is needed and no appointment has been made by the parents. In addition, courts will generally honor such testamentary appointments in the event of a family dispute.

When the parents of minor children go out of town without the children, whether they are young or teenagers, a parental power of attorney is an essential document to have in place. Such a document allows the parental attorney-in-fact to deal with medical issues, school matters, and other legal problems (*e.g.*, a run-in with the law), that could arise in the parents' absence. Even if the child is old enough to stay home for a few days without direct adult supervision, there should be someone who has the authority to act in the parents' place while they are away. Under many states' laws, parental powers of attorney are only valid for limited duration, *e.g.*, six months. The document should be witnessed and notarized and signed by both parents, if possible. It is helpful for the document to include HIPAA provisions regarding the children's medical history and current conditions.

As children under 18 cannot inherit property in most states without necessitating the creation of a conservatorship, assets that are intended to pass to a minor, either through one's Will or as a result of a life insurance or retirement plan beneficiary designation, should instead be left to the minor in trust or through a custodial arrangement under the Uniform Transfers to Minors Act (UTMA). *See* Chapters 10 and 11.

Young Adults and Their Parents

Once a child attains age 18 or is otherwise legally emancipated, he is an adult in the eyes of the law. The child's parents technically no longer have the right to the child's medical information or to make medical decisions for the child, and no longer have the right to access school or financial records (even if the parent is footing the bills). In the event a situation arises where an adult child needs help due to a situation that he is unable to manage alone, or due to a temporary absence or incapacity, the parent may not be allowed, by a given institution, to become involved absent a health care power of attorney and/or general durable power of attorney executed by the adult child naming the parent(s) as his agent(s).

Absent valid powers of attorney, or in the event the power of attorney that has been executed is insufficient to handle a certain situation, a guardianship may become necessary to appoint the person who will have legal authority to act on behalf of an incapacitated adult for personal care matters, and a conservatorship may be necessary to manage that person's financial affairs. Adult guardianships and conservatorships are expensive, time consuming, and become public record. They can be avoided with proper planning. *See* Chapter 10

In the event of a death, absent a validly executed Will, all of the assets of an unmarried adult with no children will pass to his parents. If his parents are not living, the assets will pass to his siblings. An unmarried adult who wishes to have his assets disposed of in a specific manner in the event of his death must make proper provisions through a validly executed Will.

Unmarried Adults

A single adult, whether in her 20's or 70's, faces a unique set of issues. There are certain rights sometimes afforded to the spouse of a married person that are not afforded to the partner or family members of a single person. In the event of unavailability or incapacity, without valid health care and durable general powers of attorney in place, no other person has the legal authority to act on behalf of an unmarried individual. Doctors and others may provide information to family members and allow family members to make medical decisions on behalf of an unmarried person, but they are not required to do so. In certain medical situations, non-family members will not be permitted to visit the unmarried individual irrespective of the relationship, absent a valid health care power of attorney. Fiancés, boyfriends, girlfriends, general friends, relatives, and in many cases, even spouses, have no automatic legal authority. In some situations, a guardianship may become necessary to appoint the person who will have legal authority to act on behalf of an incapacitated adult. Similarly, a conservatorship may become necessary to appoint the person who will have legal authority to manage the incapacitated adult's finances. Adult guardianships and conservatorships are expensive, time-consuming, and become public record. They are generally avoidable with appropriate documentation, however. *See* Chapter 10.

Two unmarried persons who are cohabitating should consider entering into a property management agreement. The rights of a married couple who divorce are protected, in part, by the state's divorce laws. Such laws do not protect unmarried couples who cohabit and then separate. A cohabitation agreement can help the parties set forth their rights in shared property at a time when the relationship is amicable. It can also be used to ensure the rights of one partner to continue to use the property of the other in the event the other becomes incapacitated or dies.

Beth's Story. Beth and her domestic partner Karen lived together 400 miles away from Beth's parents and her home town. Beth's parents were nice people with conservative, traditional values, who did not approve of her lifestyle and who blamed Karen for luring their daughter into an "unhealthy" relationship. When Beth died suddenly in an accident, her grief-stricken parents turned their sadness into anger against Karen, barring her from the shared apartment which was In Beth's name, taking all of Beth's possessions, making burial arrangements without notice to Karen, and speaking ill of Karen to anyone who would listen. Beth had no Will or other personal planning documents. If her parents' actions against Karen were not what she would have intended, she failed to take care of her personal business to give rights to her domestic partner.

Unmarried persons in a committed relationship should, at the very least, have Wills. State intestacy laws, *i.e.*, the laws that govern the distribution of one's property at her death absent a valid Will, provide for the distribution of an unmarried person's property to her legal family. Absent a validly executed Will, a surviving domestic partner has no right to receive property from the estate of the deceased partner and may be at the mercy of the deceased partner's family with respect to the use of the deceased partner's assets.[1] Absent specific appointment in the deceased partner's Will, the surviving partner has no right under state law to serve as the personal representative (*i.e.*, executor) of the deceased partner's estate. In addition, the deceased partner's interest in jointly owned property (unless title is designated "with right of survivorship"[2]) will become the property of her family, creating a joint ownership situation that could be awkward at best.

Finally, under most states' laws, when a married couple divorces, any provisions in one ex-spouse's Will, trust, or power of attorney pertaining to the other ex-spouse becomes ineffective as though the ex-spouse were no longer living. These provisions do not apply to unmarried couples. Thus, in the event of a termination of the relationship, the former partner is not automatically removed as a beneficiary or fiduciary in the other's estate plan. In such situations, therefore, it is essential that all existing estate planning documents be reviewed and updated as needed and without delay.

Married Adults

Although married adults are often afforded access to

---

1 The laws concerning who can marry are evolving at the time of this writing. Court cases and federal, state and local laws may alter these statements over time, but they should not be relied upon to replace the need for each person to have his own estate planning documents.
2 Assets owned as "joint tenants with right of survivorship" will generally pass to the surviving joint tenant, irrespective of the provisions of one's Will or trust.

information about each other, this access is not required by law and is not always readily given. Married couples should not assume that in the event of an incapacity or medical situation of one person that his spouse will be given full authority to act on his behalf. Many institutions, including insurance companies and financial institutions dealing with an account that is not jointly owned, will not provide a spouse with information about the other spouse's matters absent a valid general durable power of attorney or if at death, a trust or letters testamentary to act for the estate.

Married couples where one or both spouses have children from prior relationships also need to have Wills in place. Absent a Will, state law will govern which assets of the deceased spouse will be allocated to his children and which will be allocated to the surviving spouse. These state laws do not apply when the deceased spouse has a valid Will in place at the time of death. The deceased spouse's assets will pass as provided in his Will or as set forth on beneficiary designations.

Even for modest estates, a revocable living trust should be established when there are concerns about a long-term incapacity or when there will be property to be probated in more than one state or country. Avoiding probate through the use of a revocable living trust can save one's family money and effort at a time when they are grieving. *See* Chapter 4.

Divorced Adults

As stated above, under state law, when a married couple divorces, any provisions in one ex-spouse's Will, trust, power of attorney, or beneficiary designations pertaining to the other ex-spouse become ineffective as though the ex-spouse were no longer living.[3] It is nevertheless imperative

---

3 Note that state law does not remove an ex-spouse's family members if they are named as fiduciaries.

to update one's estate plan upon divorce. Otherwise, the administration of the documents by the successor fiduciary can become cumbersome and confusing and often requires court involvement. The one exception to the applicability of state laws is with federally qualified employee benefits administered under the Employee Retirement Income Security Act or "ERISA." The U.S. Supreme Court[4] has ruled that the plan's beneficiary designation at the employee participant's death will prevail, regardless of state laws regarding divorce. Therefore, it is critical for a divorced employee to consult with her human resources department or other plan administrator to update beneficiary designations on all employer-provided plans, from pension and Sec. 401(k) plans to insurance coverage. *See* also Chapter 21.

The Elderly

The elderly often need additional assistance in managing their affairs. There are a number of ways for an elderly person to structure her estate plan to be certain that the appropriate level of help is available to her as her situation changes. Having one's assets in trust ensures that if the elderly person becomes unable to manage her affairs, someone else is legally authorized to step in and begin managing the elderly person's assets without court intervention. This is done through a successor trustee designation in the self-governing trust document. There may, however, come a time when the elderly person is not ready to cede complete control over her affairs but, nevertheless, needs some assistance. By having provisions in the trust allowing the elderly person to appoint a co-trustee or execute a special power of attorney, the elderly person can delegate certain responsibilities to trusted family members without giving up complete control of her affairs. If the elderly person's assets are in trust, a general power of attorney given by the elderly person to another

---

4 *Boggs v. Boggs*, 520 US 833, 117 S. Ct. 1754 (1997). Note that the community property aspect of ownership under state tax has also been preempted by ERISA.

person that does not specifically allow the other person to act as trustee of the trust will often be insufficient for these purposes. An incapacitated person cannot execute a health care or general power of attorney. So, it is essential that these documents are executed well ahead of the time when they are actually needed.

Even with a fully funded trust in place, having a current general power of attorney in place is still very important. Absent a general power of attorney, no one will be authorized to act on the elderly person's behalf with respect to matters outside the trust, such as retirement and insurance issues, taxes, and government benefits. Similarly, a health care power of attorney is needed to ensure that there is a person who is legally authorized to make the elderly person's medical decisions if she is unable to do so herself either temporarily or on a long-term basis.

If an elderly person's assets are not in trust, a valid general power of attorney is the only way for a third person to be able to help the elderly person manage his or her financial affairs without court action. This is the case irrespective of whether the elderly person is completely incapacitated or just needs help dealing with isolated matters, such as a problem with Social Security. If the elderly person is incapacitated, absent a valid health care power of attorney or general power of attorney, a guardianship or conservatorship may become necessary to name an appropriate person to act on behalf of, and manage the assets of, the elderly person.

Planning for Special Needs

In estate planning, one is considered to have "special needs" if he receives, or may in the future receive, government benefits due to developmental or other disability. Many such benefits, such as governmental Medicaid programs, impose eligibility limits based on income and available resources.

Thus, assets that will pass from a family member to a person who has special needs should be placed in a "special needs trust" that conforms with state and federal law to avoid causing that person to lose his benefits. *See* Chapter 11, for further discussion.

Planning for Business Owners

Business owners should hold their businesses in limited liability entities such as a limited liability partnership (LLP) limited liability limited partnership, limited liability company (LLC), or corporation. Such entities protect the business owner's personal assets from most debts and liabilities of the business entity (so long as the owner has not personally guaranteed the debt). In the case of a limited liability partnership, a limited liability limited partnership, and a limited liability company, the entity also provides some protection of the business assets from the owner's personal liabilities and debts. Segregation of assets is a key component to an effective asset protection plan. Each business venture should be held in a separate entity to avoid one venture's liabilities from jeopardizing the assets of the others. Similarly, if the business owner owns a business as well as the building that the business occupies, the business and building should generally be held in separate entities to avoid the potential loss of one due to the financial problems of the other. All such entities should transact affairs at arm's length with each other and with the business owner. In other words, related entities should do business with each other as though they were unrelated. For example, where the business owner holds his business and building in separate LLCs, there should be a lease between the two entities, actual rent payments, rent tax reporting and payment, if any, etc. Each entity should maintain its own books and accounts. The business owner's personal expenses should not be paid from entity accounts. Failing to observe these formalities can jeopardize the liability protection generally offered by such entities.

16 WHAT IS A GRANTOR TRUST? DO I NEED ONE?

Like the term "trust", which references a basic concept capable of being refined with lots of features for specific purposes (revocable or irrevocable, lifetime duration or multiple generational, simple or complex, etc.), the grantor trust similarly Is useful for multiple purposes. The grantor trust concept is an income tax notion which means that the "grantor" is responsible for paying the income taxes on trust earnings. Typically, a trust itself is the taxable entity. It may pay its own taxes on income or make distributions of taxable income to the beneficiaries, who then become responsible for their portion of taxes on the trust's taxable income. With a grantor trust, however, the trust is not the taxable entity.

The grantor is usually the person who establishes the trust, who can also be called the trustor or settlor. For income tax purposes, however, the grantor can be anyone who makes a contribution to a trust which is characterized as a grantor trust. The grantor is treated as the "owner" of the trust assets contributed. Usually there is one grantor, *e.g.,* the father who transfers his stock ownership, the aunt who sets up an irrevocable life insurance trust for payment of estate taxes, etc. Being the grantor of a grantor trust can be financially meaningful if the trust owns serious income-producing assets. The grantor must be prepared to pay the taxes on trust earnings. The good news is that if the grantor pays the income taxes, he is depleting his estate by the tax amounts so that those amounts won't be subject to estate taxes at his death. On the other hand, if all the trust owns is non-income producing assets such as one or more life insurance policies, there won't be trust income to pass on to the grantor for income tax paying purposes.

There are several ways to make a trust be taxable as a grantor trust.[1] Any trust that provides for ownership of a life insurance policy insuring the grantor's life is a grantor trust. Other features also can make the trust a grantor trust. The trust can state that the grantor or another person can substitute other assets for assets in the trust; the grantor can retain a right called a revisionary interest in the value of the trust assets exceeding 5% thereof; the grantor or a "nonadverse" party can control who has beneficial enjoyment of the trust income or principal; the grantor or a nonadverse party can revoke the trust with its assets going back to the grantor; the grantor can vote securities in a related company; giving a beneficiary a withdrawal right creates a grantor trust as to the right; and the grantor or a nonadverse party can choose to distribute income to the grantor or her spouse.

It is often very desirable for a trust to have the grantor feature. When the grantor sells an asset to the grantor trust, she is selling the asset to herself for income tax purposes, so there is no tax on the sale. But, because the trust is legally

---

1 *See* IRC Sec. 671 et seq.

a separate entity, the sale will remove the asset from the grantor's estate for estate tax purposes.

A very useful tool in estate and tax planning is often referred to as an "intentionally defective grantor trust" or "IDGT" (think, "I dig it"). This is an irrevocable trust. Before trust tax rate brackets became more compressed than for individuals,[2] grantor trust treatment was often avoided, and as described above, it takes a special effort to create a grantor trust. Consequently the creation of a grantor trust is referred to as being "intentional" and in the past, the grantor feature was considered bad or "defective," hence the negative connotation of the title, an intentionally defective grantor trust. Such a trust, however, can have a great positive effect.

A sale to an IDGT can be made without income tax consequences to the grantor. If the trust has no current income until the sale is made, the grantor can receive a promissory note for the payment of the purchase price. As the trust makes payment on the promissory note, the grantor has retained an income stream from the trust property, but any appreciation in the property will be removed from her estate for estate tax purposes.

The Internal Revenue Service has not formally approved a variety of these uses of the grantor trust for the tax savings provided, and future legislation could impact their effectiveness.

Your revocable living trust is also a grantor trust, during your lifetime, but because it is revocable, it does not have the estate tax savings capabilities discussed above.

---

2 Trusts pay the same income tax rates on income as individuals do, but a trust in 2013 will hit the top income tax bracket of 39.6% at $11,950 of taxable income rather than approximately $400,000 for a single individual. Thus, most of the time, it makes economic sense to distribute trust taxable income to beneficiaries or to set up a grantor trust to avoid income taxes at the trust level.

17 SHOULD YOU USE A TRUST PROTECTOR?

Your consideration and elimination process has already been stretched to the max in coming up with names of trustees and guardians for your minor children. And your lawyer also wants to put in some "additional beneficiaries" into your life insurance trust. Now you are being asked if you want a trust protector. You thought the trustee and several successors were enough, and you are ashen over the prospect of naming someone who will oversee the trustee. You are advised, however, that since your dynasty trust will last for multiple generations, you should have trust protector language in place for maximum future flexibility.

The trust protector can have many functions, as spelled out in the trust document. As a concept imported from Britain and other common law countries, the use of trust protectors became popular in this country in the 1990s. Today, several states have trust protector statutes.[1] Powers can include modification of the trust agreement for tax purposes or to reflect changes in a beneficiary's status, approval of certain acts of the trustee, removal of the trustee, and other useful capabilities.

If you have two or three trusted people whom you will be naming as back-up trustees, you could name one of them as a current trust protector. If that person was ever needed in the trustee's position, then your successor trust protector could begin serving.

The trust protector generally does not act as a fiduciary but rather is the second set of eyes on the scene guarding the trust and also assisting the trustee and beneficiaries by recommending and implementing changes.

By the way, you could name an advisory committee as well in addition to the trust protector.

---

1 Arizona Revised Statutes Sec. 14-10818(B)(1)-(5) provides the following: "B. A trust protector appointed by the trust instrument has the powers, delegations and functions conferred on the trust protector by the trust instrument. These powers, delegations and functions may include the following: 1. Remove and appoint a trustee. 2. Modify or amend the trust instrument for any valid purpose or reason, including, without limitation, to achieve favorable tax status or to respond to changes in the internal revenue code or state law, or the rulings and regulations under that code or law. 3. Increase, decrease, modify or restrict the interests of any beneficiary of the trust. 4. Modify the terms of a power of appointment granted by the trust. 5. Change the applicable law governing the trust."

18 WHAT DOES IT MEAN TO DECANT THE TRUST?

Decanting is a term synonymous with reformation, but it can usually be done without need for a court order approving the revisions, if authorized under state laws. Irrevocable trusts cannot be amended or restated. The reference to trusts in this chapter will relate solely to irrevocable trusts or to revocable trusts which have become irrevocable upon the death or incapacity of the trustor. State statutes approving decanting often specify the reasons that an irrevocable trust can be modified and who must approve the modification. Reasons to decant a trust can include improving the structure of the trust, adding governing provisions, taking advantage of law changes, changing dispositive provisions especially if changes in the law or a beneficiary's circumstances have made the terms negative or unhelpful, and generally modernizing an old trust agreement.[1] Keep in mind that

[1] To avoid a negative impact under the generation-skipping transfer tax laws, changes made through decanting should fit within four requirements found in the GST regulations at Regs. §26.2601-1(b)(4), which are aimed at not changing a

state law may also limit or prohibit decanting, unless there is a court order for reformation.

Heirs can develop a host of changes in their circumstances. Think about your heirs as not only being your children, but also including their children and their children. If you have a 500-year long trust, you will potentially have twelve to twenty-four generations of beneficiaries. With that number of people, there can be a lot of divorces, maybe some addictions and criminal conduct, mental illness, or just generally dysfunctional relationships. A trust which will last "in perpetuity" magnifies the problem dramatically.

George's Story. George and his wife ended up adopting his sister's child Thomas when she took her own life. They raised Thomas as their own, and it was not until they went to a new lawyer who reviewed their existing estate planning documents did they realize that they had not included Thomas as a beneficiary in George's ILIT. George created the ILIT before the issue with his sister and Thomas had arisen. George's attorney suggested decanting, to change the beneficiaries of the trust to include Thomas. Other modifications due to changes in tax laws were also suggested. Bank #1 which was serving as corporate trustee was willing to decant the trust to add Thomas as a beneficiary, but it required a court order to approve the other suggested administrative revisions. George was able, under the terms of the trust agreement, to change corporate trustees, so he removed Bank #1 as trustee with a simple letter, and with a one-page document named Bank #2 as trustee. Bank #2 was happy to approve the suggested administrative revisions through decanting, and signed the new trust agreement. It remained the same trust, but after decanting, it had an additional beneficiary and updated provisions. No court order was needed.

While the trustee's powers to decant can usually be limited

---

person's beneficial interest in the trust.

will continue in its irrevocable state for many years, such as a dynasty trust, you should consider leaving those useful, time- and cost-savings decanting powers in place because life changes so frequently, and the trust needs a way to keep up with those countless changes. Limitations, however, may be inserted or prohibited in the trust agreement, if decanting is a major concern of yours.

19 POWERS OF APPOINTMENT

Irrevocable trusts are just that: unamendable, unchangeable, meant to be carved in stone, with no easy way to modify them. With new laws, it is true that even irrevocable trusts can be decanted, but often state laws with decanting provisions will limit the reasons for decanting. And, reliance on a court to approve changes that a petitioner desires in a reformation action is somewhat risky. When you create an irrevocable trust, however, whether it is a life insurance trust, a credit shelter trust, a QTIP trust, educational trust for young adults, or similar document, those trusts can last for a long time, and laws and people's circumstances can change. The power of appointment is one provision you could insert in your document which would give a beneficiary some additional rights.

The power of appointment is a provision in a Will, trust or other instrument which gives a person the ability to determine whether he or a third party can receive certain benefits from the trust, Will or other document. The power of appointment can be general, which means that the receiver of the power of appointment can appoint himself, his estate or his creditors as the recipient of the benefits. Or, it can be a special power of appointment under which the person with the power must appoint only third party recipients and not himself, his estate or his creditors.

For tax purposes, the holder of a general power of appointment is treated as owning the property subject to the power, and that property will be included in his taxable estate. The power will expire, unless earlier stated, at the death of the holder of the power, if it is not used.

A power of appointment does not have to use specific words and can be inferred from the context. It should be in writing, however, to be effective.

Joe's Story. Joe wanted to be sure that his grandchildren received his antique car collection, but at their ages, he was not sure who would want which and whether the grandchildren would be in a position in their lives to take care of them. He gave his son Paul the ability to make the decision, in his trust, as follows: "I give my son Paul the authority to determine who among my grandchildren shall receive one or more of my antique cars." In this special power of appointment, Paul cannot have a car, but he can decide who among his children, nieces, and nephews could receive the cars at Joe's death. Paul incurs no gift tax liability in implementing this special power of appointment.

A popular power of appointment is known as a "5x5" or "five by five" power. It is inserted in an irrevocable trust benefiting a surviving spouse, such as a credit shelter trust or a QTIP and provides that the spouse beneficiary has the right to take from the principal of the trust each year the sum of $5,000 or 5% of the value of the trust assets, whichever is greater. If a general power of appointment is more than the 5x5 formula, the lapse in its use may constitute a taxable gift by the surviving spouse.

There are several uses of the 5x5 power. It allows the surviving spouse to take out an amount of principal from the trust each year over and above her needs for health, education, maintenance and support without a needs determination by the trustee. In some states with separate estate taxation, it allows the surviving spouse to engage in some tax planning. And, if income is low in a particular year, the surviving spouse can augment his income with the principal withdrawal. Further, use of the 5x5 power eliminates certain taxation which is otherwise imposed if a beneficiary lets a general power of appointment lapse due to non-use.

Jake's and Jennie's Story. Jake wanted his wife Jennie to appreciate the family wealth which was based on stock he inherited from his grandparents, and he knew she would live much longer than he would, due to his health conditions. He had already used up his gift/estate tax exemptions in transferring stock to his children, so he provided in his Will that his estate would be transferred into a QTIP trust for Jennie. With the QTIP trust, she would get all of the income generated by the trust assets, and the stock was starting to throw off substantial dividends. Just in case there was a lean year, however, he had the 5x5 power inserted in the trust. Each year Jennie could take out 5% of the trust principal, in the form of stock, so that thirty years later when she was in her 80s, she owned a significant portion of the stock in her own name. In 2013, the value of the QTIP trust assets was $50,000,000. Her annual distribution of principal from the trust, the 5%, was now at $2.5 million.

The downside to using a 5x5 power is that in situations

where the power is contained in the credit shelter trust, that provision allows for the placement of previously untaxed assets squarely in the surviving spouse's estate for estate tax purposes. If that is the desired consequence, then it's a good use of the 5x5 provision.

20 HOW WILL A PRENUPTIAL AGREEMENT HELP ME?

A prenuptial agreement is a contract negotiated between two people who plan to be married. The consideration for the contract is the act of each party in marrying the other. State laws generally provide for prenuptial agreements, in case law and in their statutes. Sometimes referred to as an "antenuptial agreement" or "pre-marriage contract," the prenuptial agreement can override the usual provisions of law regarding property ownership, debts, etc., as between married persons, or the agreement can be used to strengthen established legal rules.

Each of the parties should be independently represented by an attorney prior to their signing the prenuptial agreement, so that both parties have the opportunity to understand the issues, receive information about the property owned by each other and any debts that exist, and negotiate issues important to the marriage. Some states specifically require representation by independent legal counsel for each party in order for the agreement to be enforceable. Whether or not state law requires that representation, having separate representation is essential. Divorce courts do not like being told what to do, so it is only with a well-negotiated contract between two parties with separate attorneys signing off for each of them that the parties have some assurance that in divorce, should that occur, their pre-marriage agreement terms will be upheld.

Tahiti Wedding Story. The bride-to-be was on the airplane going to Tahiti with her fiancé sitting next to her. They were arriving the day before they were to say their marriage vows on the beach surrounded by friends and family. It was all arranged: the flowers, food, champagne, band, and judge. Half the wedding party and many relatives were on the same plane with them to attend the ceremony and party afterwards. Many other friends and family members were arriving later in the day or had already landed. After the drinks had been served on the plane and the engaged couple toasted each other, the groom-to-be pulled out papers from his briefcase. "I need to have you sign this document," he said to her. "My lawyer drew it up. It's, you know, so that my stuff stays my stuff and," he sheepishly grinned, "so you can't take it all from me in case you decide to leave me." He did not say, "like my last wife did," but that was the implication. He handed her the document, which was about ten pages long, pulled out his pen, looked in her startled eyes, and said, "It's simple. Just sign it." After some tears and hurt feelings, she did sign the document, scarcely understanding anything she was reading in her hurried and upset state. They were married, had children, and the agreement was tucked away for years. Twenty nine years later, after the husband had numerous affairs and was no longer a nice person to the wife, she filed for divorce. Out came the prenuptial agreement, which said the wife would get nothing of the husband's separate property in divorce. He had kept everything of significant value separate and in his name during the marriage, and the prenuptial agreement had said that all of his earnings would be his separate property as well. Despite him supporting her for so many years, the woman did not own anything of her own from the marriage, and she was not entitled to alimony (called spousal maintenance in many states) according to the agreement. Finding that the agreement had never been properly negotiated and that the wife was the disadvantaged party forced to sign the agreement with no legal representation, the family law court threw out the entire agreement, and awarded the wife half of all of husband's property. A better written agreement, properly negotiated with representation on both sides, would have preserved the legitimate agreements of the parties. The stealth attack used by the groom-to-be was unsustainable.

A prenuptial agreement, however, is not just about spelling out what happens if the marriage fails. It can deal beneficially with many topics. In it, the parties should make clear what is each party's separately owned property and what will constitute marital or community property. Separate debts brought into the marriage by either party can be identified and protection given to the non-debtor spouse. If one spouse stops working to care for the household, agreements can be made regarding sharing of expenses, later education, property ownership, etc., so that neither party is disadvantaged. Estate planning and divorce planning can be set forth, so that a potential outcome, negotiated fairly for each party, will be available should the marriage end in either death or divorce. Time limits and periods can be arranged. For instance, a provision can state that if divorce occurs, spousal maintenance will be paid and increased for every 5 years of marriage.

While prenuptial agreements are often used in situations where the parties' incomes are uneven, they can bring a great deal of clarity and peace in a second marriage situation where there are separate children, concerns about inheritances, and property and debt issues. Tax matters can also be effectively handled through a prenuptial agreement. The parties can agree to file joint or separate tax returns, and each can agree to indemnify the other for tax liabilities. Business debt is often a big issue for married couples. With a properly crafted prenuptial agreement and appropriate property titling, one party may be able to avoid personally guaranteeing the other's business debts, leases, and other obligations.

Tax Liability Story. The couple had spent several years together unmarried because of the man's unpaid tax liabilities. The woman did not want her income to be taken by the taxing authorities. They wanted to be married, however, so they entered into a pre-marriage agreement, with separate lawyers representing each of them. In it, they provided that all property and earnings would remain separate property under state law, and that the debts they were each bringing into the marriage would remain separate. Because the IRS generally looks to and follows applicable state law provisions regarding property ownership, the IRS respected the couple's prenuptial agreement and only sought collection of the tax liabilities from the husband's property and earnings.

Prenuptial agreements can be amended or even later revoked, so long as both parties agree in writing. The prenuptial agreement provides a "default" position for each party, in the event other agreements cannot be reached. Why rely solely on legislative law to structure your property ownership and most private of relationships?

Post-Nuptial Agreements

Married couples and nonmarried parties can also enter into contracts with each other, in the form of postnuptial or property agreements, and in those cases, the consideration must be something other than marriage. For example, in consideration of neither party being responsible for the other party's separate future debt, the parties can enter into a post-marriage agreement splitting ownership of their assets, assigning debt responsibilities, and setting forth other terms they wish to agree upon.

John's and Jane's Story. John and Jane had been married for 35 years when John's latent bipolar condition reared its head in several difficult public attacks. The couple had amassed a significant net worth, and Jane was afraid most of it would be used in taking care of John. She was willing to stay married to him and provide personal care but did not want to become impoverished in the process. The parties each hired separate counsel, Jane's lawyer wrote the agreement, and John's lawyer reviewed it, conferred with John, and negotiated several points. The parties signed the finished agreement, and the assets assigned to each party in the agreement were re-titled to either Jane's or John's name respectively. When John later had to be institutionalized because he was not able to function on his own or at home anymore, John's funds were used to pay for his care, and Jane was not a financially responsible party, due to the carefully prepared and negotiated agreement.

There are many other reasons a married couple may wish to enter into such an agreement. As with the prenuptial agreement, the postnuptial agreement can override state law provisions regarding property ownership, debt responsibilities, alimony rights in the event of divorce, etc. Couples often spend tens of thousands of dollars fighting over issues in a divorce. A few thousand dollars spent earlier for a postnuptial agreement could either save the marriage by taking certain issues off the table or pave the way later for a more amiable and cheaper dissolution action.

If you cannot convince your fiancé to consider a prenuptial agreement, you should consider setting up an asset protection trust (domestic or foreign) or even just a revocable living trust before you marry. Having your own separate property trust will help identify your separate property, its appreciation, ownership, and your decision-making capabilities concerning your separate property, particularly if you have a business, from your spouse's reach unless he has a legal claim against you. You and your selected trustee would make all decisions about investments, distributions, business operations, etc. Your assets would be better protected from your spouse's debts and from his ability to share in those assets in the event of divorce. And, of course, having the revocable living trust as a single person, before getting a fiancée, makes a lot of sense from a personal planning standpoint.

21 DIVORCING? Here's What ELSE You Need to Do...

You have just had a fractious, expensive divorce. You are tired of lawyers, fees, papers, dealing with your ex, etc. There are, however, very serious matters which you still must handle for your future financial and legal well-being. If your post-divorce debris is not handled properly, major problems can occur. Most divorce attorneys do not include handling property and business matters as part of their divorce services in assisting clients to terminate their marriages, settle child custody disputes, etc. If you have recently gotten a divorce or if you never did anything following your divorce years ago, the following steps should be taken without delay.

1. **Qualified Domestic Relations Order ("QDRO")** – This order is needed if your ex has a pension plan and you are to get part of it. The court must issue a qualified domestic relations order, or "QDRO," directing a pension plan to pay you your share of pension funds as a

non-participant former spouse if plan assets are awarded in the divorce decree. QDROs are often not part of the divorce procedure. It is up to you to get a QDRO. For example, if the divorce decree states that you are to receive one-third of the pension plan value accumulated to the date of the divorce, then the QDRO is needed to direct the plan administrator to determine what that value is of the participating spouse's share of the pension plan, and pay it out to you or transfer it to an individual retirement account (IRA) of your choice. Without the QDRO, the plan administrator cannot, by law, act to deplete the participant spouse's plan share. Some family law attorneys will provide QDRO services, and others will not, often depending on the practice customs in each state or location. The parties are often referred to tax attorneys for preparation of the QDRO. You need to find an attorney willing to help prepare and secure your QDRO.

QDRO Story. The wife's attorney represented her through a difficult divorce from a man who was full of lies and deceit. He nevertheless held responsible jobs and had built up a sizable retirement account. The attorney decided to handle the QDRO himself which should have been easy because the court had awarded half the pension from the husband's employer to the wife. The pension plan administrator rejected the QDRO, however, because the pension plan at that employer was empty. The ex had lied to the wife, attorneys, and the court and actually had pension funds which he had acquired during marriage in two other companies' plans where he had previously worked. After the QDRO had been rejected by the plan administrator, the ex rolled the other plan account balances to his new employer's plan. The client waited three years to try to go after the pension plan assets, and by then, needed to engage a new lawyer because her prior one had retired. The original divorce decree had to be amended to include the other companies' plans, and then an amendment to the original QDRO could be obtained. While she was tired to death of the divorce wrangling, the delay in proceeding cost her not only much more in fees in getting new counsel involved but also in the use of the pension funds which were rightfully hers. Eventually she received close to $100,000 as her share of her ex's pension plan accumulations and growth.

2. **Estate Planning.** Most states' laws are clear that after a divorce, provisions for an ex-spouse in a Will or other document are void, unless you confirm your intention to name the ex-spouse in writing after the divorce. Administering your Will or trust at your death, with the ex-spouse still named in it, can be unwieldy at best. It pits your ex against your family, creates problems regarding minor children, is legally complicated, and leads to results often not intended. Life is fragile and unpredictable, and no one of us knows at what point we will die or even become incapacitated. So, redo your Will or trust, general power of attorney and health care power of attorney immediately! As with QDROs, divorce attorneys often will not do post-decree clean up. An estate planning attorney will readily see what needs to be done. While your family and friends will be upset over your demise, they will be able to mourn your passing without trying to iron out the issues in a difficult legal proceeding.

Ken's and Lisa's Story. Ken and Lisa divorced after a number of years of marriage, leaving Lisa with two small children to care for. Needless to say, Lisa's traditional Hawaiian family was no longer on good terms with the ex-son-in-law. Six months after the divorce, Lisa died suddenly. Neither she nor Ken had arranged to terminate and re-do their joint revocable living trust. Nor had the couple transferred property ownership out of the trust into their own names or into new trusts following the divorce. Lisa's elderly father, as the statutory executor of his daughter's estate, had to travel from Hawaii to the mainland several times to work on his daughter's estate settlement, to negotiate care of the minor children with his ex-son-in-law, and to institute court proceedings to claim certain of the daughter's employee benefits for the children. Had Lisa changed her beneficiaries on her life insurance and work benefits, re-titled her property, and executed a new Will, all as part of her post-divorce steps, much of her father's work would have been easier, a matter of paperwork only, and far less stressful. Also, she could have named someone else to be responsible for the estate settlement, thereby sparing her aged father the burden of serving as her executor.

3. **Beneficiary Designations.** State laws may provide that if your ex is named as a beneficiary on your life insurance, pension plan, IRA, annuity, pay-on-death account, etc., the ex cannot claim the benefits unless you re-name her as beneficiary after the divorce. Note, however, with any employer-provided policy or plan governed by the Employment Retirement and Income Security Act ("ERISA"), federal law trumps state law. The U.S. Supreme Court has ruled that with any employer-provided ERISA benefit, whoever is named is the correct beneficiary regardless of state law provisions. So if you have a pension plan through your work and your ex is still listed as the beneficiary at your death, your ex will get the benefits, not your children, your current spouse, or anyone else. These results can be catastrophic, so it is essential to make those beneficiary designation changes without delay.

Hospital Employee Story. The man had two ex-wives, an adult daughter with the first one, no children with the second one, and a current girlfriend who had two small children with him. He worked for a hospital network as a senior orderly and had substantial benefits: pension, 401(k), life insurance, health insurance, etc. When he started working for the hospital during his second marriage, he filled out the usual HR paperwork and never thought of it again. He was so glad to move on after that second marriage ended in divorce that he vowed never to marry again. One day leaving work, he and his motorcycle were hit by a red-light-running car and instantly killed. Because he had never bothered to change his beneficiary designations, federal law required that his ERISA plan benefits be paid to the second wife who was named as the beneficiary, even though they were divorced and he had dependent children. The only benefit his three children received was the life insurance policy for $36,000, since the employer-provided life insurance was not part of ERISA, and state law states that upon divorce, a named, but now former spouse is no longer entitled to be the beneficiary. Had he made changes to his beneficiary designations immediately following the divorce, the second ex-wife would have received nothing, rather than getting approximately $400,000. She refused to disclaim any part of the fund saying that God wanted her to have it all.

4. **Tax Issues.** If you and your ex signed joint income tax returns in the past or failed to file tax returns, you are both still personally liable for any unpaid tax obligations. Your settlement agreement or divorce decree should include some provisions about who is responsible for the taxes, but those documents often do not. Divorce attorneys can take the position that they cannot give tax advice, so you may be faced with a battle with the IRS or the state revenue department. The outcome and who pays will depend on the facts and circumstances of each case, but it is important for you to be responsive to the taxing authority and get the matter worked out. Keep in mind that the taxing authority will still look to both you and your ex for all of the payment, since you are jointly and severally liable for the tax. That phrase, "jointly and severally" means each of you is responsible for the whole debt. When you sign a joint tax return, you become jointly and severally liable for the debt, generally speaking, with some exceptions. But, your divorce settlement agreement is an enforceable contract between you and your ex so if the taxing authorities come after you for payment, and if you negotiated that your ex should be the responsible party, you have rights to sue your ex for the tax debt. And remember that

if you took the first-time home buyer credit, the obligations for the credit pass to the one of you who gets the home. If it is turned into a rental, then the recipient spouse must pay back the credit to the IRS in full.

Betty's Story. Betty developed pre-cervical cancer at age 36, a year after being divorced and getting custody of her four children. She also worked a responsible job which paid her benefits and provided a modest income for herself and the children. The father of the children did not always pay his child support on time. A year after the divorce, the IRS contacted Betty about back taxes owed for a prior year in which she signed a joint tax return with her husband. The IRS had evidence that he had manipulated his business expenses and had not included all business earnings in reporting income. The IRS could not locate the husband, but there Betty was, readily available with a full-time job, and fully liable for the recalculated tax debt, including penalties and interest. She attempted to negotiate with the IRS on her own, but was not able to arrange a reasonable payment plan. She did not qualify for "innocent spouse" status, because while she had no idea what the husband was doing, she benefited (presumably) from his earnings. She spent several thousand dollars hiring legal counsel to negotiate a reasonable payment plan with the IRS, which took into account her high out-of-pocket medical costs, and the attorney, knowing her rights, was able to convince the IRS to proceed also after the ex-husband. There was nothing in the divorce decree requiring the husband to take on the full tax debt or to reimburse her for any amounts she is paying to the IRS or to the attorney who represented her in the IRS negotiations.

5. **Other Matters.** After divorce, be sure to change the deeds and other titles to assets awarded to you. Recording the divorce decree is NOT a valid means to change title. There are many other types of property issues each person may need to deal with, considering each person's unique circumstances.

For instance, if one of you is awarded the house and takes over the mortgage payment and later defaults, both spouses will have severe black marks on their credit reports. If the spouse getting the house cannot afford to refinance the mortgage to remove the nonrecipient spouse's name, make sure the house is sold so that the joint mortgage liability is eliminated. Make a checklist of all of your asset and debt issues so you can address them during and after the divorce. And, don't forget to enter into a prenuptial agreement before your next marriage or a partnering agreement if you have an informal living arrangement.

Michael's and Donna's Story. The couple set up an irrevocable life insurance trust for estate tax savings purposes to hold two policies on the husband's life, naming his sister as the trustee. They made premium payments each year. In the divorce, they forgot about the legal ramifications of having the policies owned by an irrevocable trust, and the divorce decree awarded one of the policies to the husband and the other one to the wife. Donna told the trustee to cash in her policy and to give her the money which was the cash surrender value. Michael told the insurance agent on "his" policy to change the policy owner and beneficiaries to be the couple's two adult daughters. The life insurance agent, sensing something was amiss, contacted the couple's former estate planning attorney. After conferencing with all of the parties, including the trustee and the two daughters, the attorney prepared a family agreement, valid under applicable state law, which dissolved the life insurance trust, gave the cash from one policy to the wife, and gave the husband's policy to the daughters. The family agreement was necessary to settle all of the parties' respective rights, including the rights of the daughters as beneficiaries of the trust, and to enable the insurance companies to allow the changes to the policies.

Solutions are available to many issues facing divorced partners. Proper identification of the issues and addressing them in a timely manner will facilitate the process and avoid costly missteps.

22 ASSET PROTECTION

If you have ever had any sort of creditor claim against you, you know how frightening it can feel when you think about the scope of financial ruin you could face if that creditor got everything he claimed. The fear becomes maddening when you believe the claim is frivolous, false, or unfounded or simply a molehill and not the mountain being created by the creditor's word. Whether you are responsible for damages or not, your ability to move forward, think clearly, resolve the dispute on reasonable terms, and move on with your life will depend in large part on your prior asset protection planning and the completeness thereof.

Many people believe the only way to engage in asset protection planning is to move money and assets offshore into protected jurisdictions. While going off-shore is certainly one aspect of asset protection, there are many things which should be done here at home first, by everyone, even if you don't have the wherewithal to park a nest egg in an exotic non-U.S. location.

Asset protection can take many forms. The phrase refers to preventing creditors with judgments from seizing a person's real and personal property in satisfaction of the judgment claim. People are sued for many reasons, some legitimate claims as well as frivolous or vengeful actions. Insurance does not always cover every claim, and many times, claims will exceed insurance coverage limits. A $2 million umbrella policy on a client's home and cars will not provide enough protection in a $7 million car accident claim, which could happen in a fatality situation. Having appropriate asset protection planning in place, however, can enable the person on the wrong end of a lawsuit to better negotiate settlement, make plans for payment, wait for the judgment to expire, avoid bankruptcy, or otherwise fend off the sudden seizure of property. And, the umbrella insurance policy is a must to have, as a first line of defense.

To start with, state and federal laws offer some vital asset protection. For example, creditors may not seize qualified retirement plan funds, while the funds remain in the qualified plan. Many states have creditor protection statutes for IRAs, life insurance and annuity policies, a certain amount of equity in one's home (the so called "homestead exemption"), and small amounts of personal property.

Trusts with spendthrift provisions can protect trust assets held for non-grantor beneficiaries. The credit shelter trust and qualified terminable interest property trust can also provide asset protection once the grantor-spouse has died. Other types of irrevocable trusts can protect a grantor's assets so that they are held for the benefit of his heirs, without worry about the grantor's potential creditors.

Limited liability companies, limited liability partnerships, and limited partnerships, under many states' laws, will offer excellent creditor protection. Clients should determine in which states to establish their entities and engage in laddered planning. For example, a Delaware LLC owned by an Arizona limited liability limited partnership can give a great deal of protection to the assets owned in the LLC.

Domestic asset protection trusts have become popular in the last decade, and while their effectiveness has not been fully tested in the courts, such trusts can be used in conjunction with other asset protection devices.

Offshore asset protection planning can provide a number of different benefits to clients, including the ability to invest in financial markets otherwise closed to U.S. citizens. Working with established trust companies in secure jurisdictions will provide the best administration and protection for client funds and investments as well as insure that their non-U.S. assets cannot be seized by creditors.

But, beware: all states have adopted some form of the Uniform Fraudulent Conveyances Act, legislation which makes it illegal to purposefully hide assets from known legitimate creditors. Clients must verify that they are engaged in asset protection planning prospectively rather than acting in violation of any fraudulent conveyance law.

Josie's Story. Josie owned a successful import business purveying exotic food stuffs to local hotels and resorts. She was in her early 70's and had run the company for many years with her now-deceased husband. Her lawyer talked her into titling the business in a limited liability company ("LLC") as part of her estate plan. She wasn't sure about why that was done, but it was an inexpensive process and she trusted the lawyer. One day while heading home from a long day at her business facility, she entered an intersection on a green light and rammed a car which was also crossing the intersection on the perpendicular street. An ambulance nearby may have inadvertently set both directional lights to green. The driver of the other car, a 40-year-old surgeon, was instantly killed. Josie was devastated. She also feared losing her business. A lawsuit for 10 million dollars was filed against her. One look at her business held in an LLC and at the few other liquid assets she had convinced the plaintiff to settle for her car and umbrella insurance limits. The LLC gave her bargaining power which she otherwise would not have had in this difficult, emotionally charged situation.

23 FORMS OF BUSINESS ENTITIES

In the United States, most forms of business entities are created and governed by statute, usually at the state level, and in some cases by the Internal Revenue Code. Some business entity types are centuries old, while others are of modern vintage. The outline below sets forth the basic legal and federal tax characteristics of popular and legally recognized business entities. A tax and business attorney can best advise you as to the best choice for your business entity. Most of these entities will be discussed in greater detail in following the chapters.

A. Sole Proprietorship

1. Owner — One person (can include one's spouse)

2. Taxation — Business income is reported at the federal level on the owner's personal tax return (form 1040, Schedule C)

3. Liability — 100% against the owner, including acts of employees

B. General Partnership

1. Owner — Two or more persons or entities

2. Taxation —

   a. Partnership income flows through to the partners, *i.e.,* the partnership does not pay tax, only the partners do

   b. The partnership for federal tax purposes files an informational return (Form 1065) and issues Schedules K-1 to partners

   c. Partners are taxed on partnership taxable income even if the money is retained by the partnership and not distributed

   d. Partners pay self-employment taxes on partnership income generated from active business

3. Liability — 100%, joint and several among partners[1]

4. Documentation — Partners should have a written partnership agreement to define the rights and responsibilities of the partners to the partnership and to each other

5. Legal Requirements — no formal filing is needed except that states may require registration of a fictitious name

---

1 Some states have provisions for registering a general partnership as a limited liability partnership that protects the general partners from personal liability for the entity.

C. Limited Partnership

1. Owner — One or more general partners and one or more limited partners

2. Taxation — Same as general partnership

3. Liability

    a. General Partners — Complete, joint and several among general partners[2]

    b. Limited Partners — Limited to extent of initial and subsequent investments in the partnership

    c. Limited partners cannot participate in management or limited liability is lost

4. Documentation —

    a. Certificate of Limited Partnership must be filed with the applicable state authority for limited liability to be effective

    b. Need to have written limited partnership agreement for proper partner designations

D. Corporation

1. Owner — Corporation owns the business; shareholders own the corporation

2. Taxation —

    a. "C" corporation files federal Form 1120 and is taxed on its income; deduction is made

---

2 Some states have provisions for registering the entity as a limited liability limited partnership that protects the general partner from personal liability for the entity's debts.

for salaries paid to employees (including shareholder-employees) but no deduction for income distributed to shareholders in the form of dividends

b. Shareholders are taxed on salaries paid to them by the corporation if they are also employees and on dividends received

c. The taxation of income at both the corporate level and then at shareholder level distributed as dividends is referred to as "double taxation"

d. "S" Corporations -- certain corporations can elect to be taxed in a manner similar to partnerships to eliminate double taxation

e. Incorrectly formed or lapsed corporations may still be taxed as corporations under "association" status in the Code but liability protection for shareholders will be lost under state law

3. Liability —

a. Corporation — 100%

b. Shareholders — Limited solely to extent of investment in corporate stock and capital contributions, unless they misuse corporation in fraudulent or criminal actions

c. Board of Directors and Officers -- Limited except for fraud, criminality, and undeposited employee income tax and FICA withholdings

4. Documentation —

   a. Articles of Incorporation and related documents must be filed with applicable state authority to commence its existence

   b. Many formalities must be observed including annual meetings, filing annual reports, etc. in order to maintain corporate status

   c. S Corporation must file federal Form 2553 with IRS within 75 days of its first day of existence or beginning of calendar year for change in tax status

E. Limited Liability Company

1. Owner — One or more members

2. Taxation — Entity chooses how to be taxed: sole proprietor with one member; partnership with more than one member; C corporation; or with election, S corporation

3. Liability — Member's liability is generally limited to the extent of initial and subsequent investments in the entity; member's interest in the LLC can be creditor protected under some states' laws

4. Documentation —

   a. Articles of Organization or similarly titled document must be filed with the applicable state authority to commence

   b. Fewer legal formalities than with a corporation

    c. Operating Agreement (or similarly titled document) recommended

F. Business Trust

A trust is not an appropriate form of entity with which to conduct a business. Trusts are taxed on earnings at extremely unfavorable tax rates. A Business Trust Organization ("BTO") must be formed as a corporation under state law or it is not a separate entity. Unscrupulous salespeople market BTO packages for tax benefits. The use of trusts as business entities is scrutinized by the IRS, and audit risks are increased dramatically.

24 FAMILY LIMITED PARTNERSHIP

Prior to the development of the limited liability company and other entities with liability limitations, the limited partnership ("LP") has been utilized for many years as an effective tool to hold and protect assets, achieve discounts, provide a gifting mechanism to family members, and remove assets or at least the appreciation on those assets from the partnership creator's estate. Even today, many practitioners prefer the family limited partnership ("FLP") over the LLC, for its history and well-established rules. The newness of LLCs often makes it difficult to determine how the IRS and the courts will interpret a particular use of an LLC. Presumably it's just like the FLP, but there is no certainty. Also, in states that have less favorable asset protection provisions for the LLC interests and its assets, the FLP offers time-honored security. The structure of the FLP, however, can be limiting or require special protective steps. Note that all family limited partnerships are limited partnerships, but not all limited partnerships have exclusively all family members as partners, which makes them family limited partnerships.

All limited partnerships ("LPs"), including FLPs, are made up of a general partner and limited partners, as two separate classes of membership. An LP (including the FLP) must be specially registered in the state of formation in order to have the limited liability feature. Otherwise, the entity is only a general partnership, with no liability protection for the partners. The LP's general partner usually holds a very small interest in the LP, such as 1%, but that is a flexible number. The general partner is responsible for all maintenance, management and running of the partnership and is personally responsible for all debts of the partnership. Often a protective entity such as an LLC will be set up to be the general partner, so that partnership debts will not become liabilities of any one individual.[1] The limited partners, on the other hand, enjoy freedom from liability for debts of the partnership, but their role in the functioning of the partnership must be very limited in order to maintain their unique protection. A limited partner who reaches too far afield and becomes active as a managing partner in the entity will risk being held responsible for partnership debts.

Tax-wise, the limited partnership must follow the tax rules for partnerships, meaning that the entity is a flow-through entity. All partners must include their proportionate share of the net income of the partnership on their individual tax returns. The federal partnership return, Form 1065, is referred to as an informational return. On the 1065, the partnership reports the income and expenses it has incurred for the year, and then the taxable income and unique expense items are reported to each partner on a Schedule K-1. The partner places those items on his individual federal income tax return, Form 1040 or its various schedules.

---

1 In some states, a general partner is afforded liability protection by registering the limited partnership as a limited liability limited partnership.

If a limited partner has a personal creditor apart from the limited partnership who has obtained a judgment against the limited partner, that creditor's only way to satisfy the creditor's claim is to get a "charging order" from the court against the limited partner's interest in the limited partnership, under the LP laws of most states. The charging order against a limited partnership for a debtor limited partner is the same concept and type as the charging order against an LLC member's interest as further discussed in the LLC materials herein. In fact, the LP charging order concept was devised many years before LLCs were created in the law, and the charging order provisions were essentially copied into the LLC laws. As noted, not all LLC statutes have the most protective language for their charging orders, but LP charging orders are generally uniform across the states.[2]

So what's all the fuss about the family limited partnership? It has been a very effective estate planning tool for many years. But, as abuses mounted on top of abuses, the IRS became very aggressive in attacking estates where the decedent had an interest in an FLP and had been the person who set it up, funded it, and gave FLP interests to his children. For those cases in which the IRS won, the entire holdings of the FLP were included in the deceased's estate for estate tax purposes. But, the IRS has not always won, and the FLP remains a useful planning tool. Without going through the torturous discussion of the cases and who did what to whom, we can look at a list of "do's and don'ts" as a useful checklist for how best to utilize the FLP for avoiding estate tax inclusion of the FLP interest or property held in the FLP.

The very first point is just that: have a better reason than estate tax avoidance for setting up the FLP for your heirs. In each case in which the taxpayer won, there was strong

---

2 The Uniform Limited Partnership Act of 2001 ("ULPA") provides the following language with respect to charging orders: under a charging order a creditor only has the rights of a transferee, and obtaining the charging order under the provisions at Sec. 703 is the sole remedy of the creditor. The ULPA has been adopted in most states with minor changes.

evidence that the FLP was set up for a much broader purpose: protecting the valuable family asset (*e.g.,* the farm or ranch), providing a means to continue the active family business, etc. Next, the limited partnership should adhere to business formalities, such as separateness of funds, earnings from assets flowing into the partnership, active management, accountings, and other things which indicate a business is being conducted. And, the FLP should not own all of the decedent's assets.

As for the "don'ts," the following features for FLPs were successfully attacked by the IRS:

- The FLP was established when the transferor was on his death bed;

- The assets placed in the FLP were passive (like stock investments) and not active in nature (which a family business would be);

- Personal use assets such as the patriarch's home were put into the FLP;

- All of the assets were put into the FLP by the matriarch leaving no non-FLP personal use assets;

- All of the matriarch's money was put into the FLP, leaving no funds available to pay her personal living expenses, including expenses of last illness and estate taxes;

- Most distributions of partnership earnings were made disproportionately back to the entity's creator; and

- Written communications, illustrations, etc. introduced at trial supported the argument that estate and income tax avoidance was the primary purpose of using the FLP (watch those emails).

In all of these types of cases, the IRS was able to effectively use the provisions of IRC sec. 2036 to pull the assets back into the estate for estate tax calculations.[3] Since most transferors want to continue to be included in the family enterprise, they are "retaining an interest," thereby opening up their estates to IRS attack. Other safeguards (steps contrary to those listed above) will work to keep the partnership outside of the transferor's estate, but one surefire way to manage the situation is to have the transferor completely devolve out of the partnership before death, particularly if most of the interests have been transferred to family members by gift rather than by sale. A valid sale is an exception to IRC sec. 2036. It has also been suggested by several commentators that a flawed FLP might be saved by having the partners sell their interests in the FLP, hence transferring the entire FLP, to an "intentionally defective grantor trust" ("IDGT") in an effort to surround the FLP with another protective device. This is a strategy which may be worth considering in some situations.

Despite the risks and often the furor created in using the FLP, or even the LLC in similar circumstances, these two protective entities are useful and legally recognized tools which are effective in reducing the risks of liabilities, curbing tax liabilities, and providing a means to control assets and gifting in ways that cannot be achieved with the assets directly.

---

3 IRC Sec. 2036 reads, "Transfers with a retained life estate will be included in the decedent's gross estate."

25 LIMITED LIABILITY COMPANY

A Limited Liability Company, or "LLC" for short, is a legal entity created under the laws of a state of the organizer's choice. All fifty states have LLC laws, but the terms often vary widely from state to state. Choosing a specific state for organization can be very important for accomplishing your goals.

The LLC is a relatively new form of organization[1] which offers many of the advantages of a partnership, limited partnership and corporation. It has quickly become the business structure of choice for many purposes, including small businesses, joint ventures, real estate or other types of syndications, and as an alternative to the family limited partnership to be a tool for family wealth protection and transfer. Unlike a limited partnership[2] in which the general partner

---

1 Wyoming had the first LLC laws in the U.S. in 1977, but it was not until the 1990s when the other states enacted their LLC statutes. Corporations, on the other hand, have been around for centuries, with the first corporations being the British East India Company, chartered in 1600, and the Dutch East India Company following in 1602.

2 *See* the preceding chapter regarding limited partnerships

will always be liable for all partnership debts, without special registration if applicable at all, the LLC laws generally provide that no member or manager of a limited liability company will be subject to liability for the activities of the company.

The LLC offers a unique blend of the legal and tax benefits which make it an attractive form of doing business. From a tax perspective the federal tax laws provide huge flexibility to the LLC. The LLC can choose any type of federal income tax treatment it wishes: as a "disregard entity" (sole proprietorship or corporate division) if it has only one member, or if the LLC has more than one member, as a "partnership." Further, regardless of the number of members, the LLC can select to be a "C corporation," and from there, if its members are qualified, it can make the election to be taxed as an "S corporation." Many states allow the same type of flexibility, but a few states depart from the federal rules and tax LLCs as corporations for all purposes.

Income-producing assets and assets with appreciation potential, such as the family farm, can be contributed to the LLC with the estate planning objective of reallocating such assets to the intended heirs, perhaps your children. The LLC also provides features for allowing a tremendous amount of flexibility to meet changing circumstances, including the ability to select who has control of your family's wealth in the event you are unable to manage your affairs.

The LLC role in estate and wealth planning also includes its use an effective technique to transfer wealth to your heirs through use of an annual gifting program. The courts and the IRS have determined that gifts of LLC interests in which the donees can actively own the interests and benefit from them are considered present interest gifts, as opposed to future interest gifts, and, therefore, are eligible for the annual gift tax exclusion. [3]

and family limited partnerships.
3 But see the case of *Hackl v. CIR*, 118 TC 279 (2002); aff'd 335 F3d 664 (7th Cir. 2003) in

The heart of the LLC's effectiveness as a valuable gifting technique is that it places the asset, such as your family's farm into an entity and fragments the entity ownership into multiple undivided interests. The underlying asset value of the farm remains the same and is free to appreciate in value. With the LLC, however, the owner/donor is able to make use of valuation strategies and leveraging opportunities not available in a living trust arrangement. The advantages of gifting LLC interests become more appealing in terms of cost effectiveness when viewed in light of the valuation discounts that are available.

As soon as cash, real estate or any other asset is placed under the umbrella of an LLC ownership, its appeal as a marketable asset to third parties diminishes. Few people will pay top dollar for a minority or non-voting interest in a company with many ownership restrictions. Since the LLC ownership is fragmented into undivided interests, your heirs have little or no individual control over the disposal of the LLC interests and no control of the management of the assets if you are the manager of the LLC. Added together, the lack of marketability, the lack of control, and the restrictions on transferring or disposing the interest, can result in valuation discounts of the LLC interests totaling as much as 30% to 50% for tax purposes (which discount supposedly matches the reduced market price due to the fractionalized ownership of LLC memberships).[4]

The ability to alter the value of an asset held in an LLC and obtain valuation discounts for tax purposes represents a unique opportunity for tax planning. The transfer of easily valued and publicly traded assets into an LLC converts the assets into non-marketable interests with substantially less apparent value.

which gifts of an LLC owning a tree farm were made to many beneficiaries and treated as future interest gifts for gift tax purposes. The terms of ownership were too restrictive to allow the beneficiaries any current enjoyment of economic benefits of ownership.
4 Note that allowable discounts for healthy marketable securities held in an LLC are not as great.

There are also non-tax consequences of these gifts. First, by transferring gifts of LLC interests, you, as the manager, can dispose of your value in the underlying asset yet retain, with some cautions, the ability to control the entire holdings. Any LLC interest that you still own at your death will certainly be less than the total value of the asset that you started out with and thus subject to a smaller amount of estate tax.

Second, your heirs do not have much more than a percentage ownership in the asset. They cannot sell, trade, or convert their interests into money or other consumable goods and squander your family's wealth away. Until the LLC dissolves, the assets are liquidated, and the proceeds distributed to all your heirs, your heirs are only entitled to their pro rata share of any distributable cash flow that you may or may not wish to provide to them from the income of the LLC assets. You may name managers to take over management of the LLC at your death or incapacity, with approval of a vote of the members as set forth in the Operating Agreement.

Third, all LLC members (presumably your family members) are protected from any liability that the LLC itself may incur. This is because ownership of an LLC interest is similar to owning shares in a corporation or limited partnership interests. Shareholders and limited partners generally have no personal liability for the debts of the underlying company. In addition, a creditor of the LLC may not recover from a member's personal assets if the LLC's assets are insufficient to satisfy the creditor's claim. Even though you would be named as the manager of the LLC, you are not liable for debts or claims against the LLC (unlike the general partner in a limited partnership).

Fourth, under many states' laws, a creditor of an LLC individual member cannot seize the LLC assets in satisfaction of the creditor's claim against the member. This can be one of the main advantages of an LLC, that it helps to protect the underlying asset from claims of the members' creditors. Assets that would ordinarily be appealing to a creditor suddenly become very undesirable when transferred into an LLC. Since an LLC interest is treated as intangible personal property, no member has an actual ownership interest in a specific piece of LLC property. The transferee owns only a percentage interest in the LLC. In a properly structured LLC, a member's creditors cannot attach the underlying assets of the LLC, nor can the creditor be substituted in as a member and obtain voting rights. State statutes which provide that the sole remedy a creditor has against the member is to obtain a "charging order" against the debtor's LLC interest offer the best asset protection. The underlying reason to only allow a charging order as a remedy is to prevent an unnecessary interruption of LLC business and also to avoid any adverse impact upon the non-debtor members in the sole remedy statutes, the creditor cannot force a foreclosure on the asset or a liquidation of the LLC. The creditor's only remedy will be the right to receive an LLC member's income or assets from the LLC if and when the manager decides to make any such distribution to the members. The manager determines the amount and timing of any distributions, so the creditor could possibly receive a holding of little value. Since the creditor cannot become a substitute member and is merely an assignee, the creditor has no voting or management participation rights. The ultimate drawback for a creditor is that the creditor, as an assignee of the debtor's interest, is now treated as the owner of that interest portion for tax purposes and must report and pay income taxes on that portion's allocated share of LLC income, even if money or property has not been distributed outright to the creditor. Therefore, the creditor runs the risk of receiving "phantom" taxable income from the LLC without ever receiving any actual distribution from the LLC. Most creditors do not want to take a "sit and wait" attitude when trying to collect on a judgment. Nor do they want to be held liable for taxes on something they do not have. Since an LLC interest is generally an undesirable and unreachable holding, creditors are usually discouraged from obtaining this type of judgment. Unfortunately, not all states have this charging order exclusivity, and not all states limit the scope of the charging order, so care must be taken in selecting a state with good creditor protection language in its LLC statutes.

An LLC is formed by filing a document often called "Articles of Organization" with the designated state authority, usually the Secretary of State or a branch thereof. Next, you and all your heirs or other LLC members should sign a document frequently called an "Operating Agreement." The Operating Agreement contains the agreed-upon provisions regarding the internal activities of the LLC, such as the rights and responsibilities of managers and members, voting rights, profit and loss allocations and distributions, transferability restrictions, and withdrawal and dissolution provisions. The Operating Agreement is not filed with any agency nor made a part of the public record. The provisions of the Operating Agreement can provide you with other types of control, including making management decisions and establishing investment policies.

A 2004 federal bankruptcy court case in Colorado made a significant change in the protection provided to certain LLCs by state statute.[5] That case involved a single-member LLC, and the court held that the charging order rules in the state statute did not apply to a single member LLC, thereby allowing the Trustee to take the member's place as owner of the LLC and its assets. Even though Colorado statutory law is not as strict as some other states' laws (such as Delaware, Nevada, Arizona, and others) in that it permits the court to impose other remedies besides the charging order, the bankruptcy court's decision has now become the law of the land at least in bankruptcy proceedings. As a creeping consequence, there are several commentators who believe that single-member

5 *In re Ashley Albright*, 291 BR 538, Bkr. D Colo. 2003.

LLCs will not protect assets against general creditors even in a non-bankruptcy situation. Despite these adverse rulings and opinions, the LLC is still a vital and important tool to use for many types of planning.

In summary, the LLC can provide the following advantages:

1. The nature of the LLC is such that it can continue to provide great protection from an individual's creditors, with adequate planning, thus further preserving the asset for the next generation.

2. You, as manager, retain the control and the authority regarding the investment and use of the assets owned by the LLC.

3. You can reduce your taxable estate by making annual gifts of LLC interests without relinquishing control of the farm or other valuable asset.

4. The annual gifts of undivided LLC interests allow the farm or other asset to continue to be managed as a single investment.

5. Gifts of LLC interests may encourage the donees (the younger generation) to be productive participants in the family business without your total loss of control.

6. You can plan for retirement by gradually transferring responsibility for the business operations or investment management, as the case may be, to the next generation and still retain an income stream.

7. If a donee of an LLC interest is subject to a lower income tax rate than you, then the income from the gifted interest will be taxed at a lower rate also, thereby further reducing the overall tax bite on LLC earnings.

8. The value of the LLC interest in your estate may be significantly discounted for estate tax purposes due to reduced values for lack of marketability and minority interest.

9. The LLC operating agreement may be drafted with certain buy-sell provisions that will insure that the interests, and thus the underlying assets, will remain within the family.

10. Since the asset is owned by an LLC, there would be no need to probate the asset upon your death, although the LLC interest may go through probate if your interest is not held in your living trust. For real estate owned through the LLC, probate would treat the interest as personal property, thereby probably eliminating a double probate and estate taxes payable to two states, your primary state of residence and where the property is located.

You may also find that, under your state laws, it is very easy and seamless to convert from your old corporate format to an LLC, without changing the company's identity for tax purposes.

26 CORPORATIONS

Everyone it seems knows the word "corporation" and its various synonyms: inc., incorporated, company, limited, ltd., etc., but what does it mean to have a corporation and should you have one? Before the days of limited liability companies, everyone in business either had a corporation or a partnership or went "bare" (no liability protection) with a sole proprietorship. Today there are more choices, for more flexibility and for good or bad, more decisions to make. Consistent with the other messages in this book, keep in mind that your decision-making should not be in a vacuum; you need the help of professionals who are trained in the rules and practicalities of tax and legal choices. Yes, everyone can set up a corporation. It involves just filling out a form and filing it with the Secretary of State's office in your state of choice, but there are a lot of intricacies to know about and think about as it relates to you. In incorporating, you have created a separate person under the law, and there are many rules of governance to be aware of.

A corporation is set up under the terms of state statutory laws. The basics are the same for each state, but there are differences to be aware of. The Articles of Incorporation, as the creating document is often called, needs to set forth the name, address, statutory agent for the corporation, and number of shares authorized. Most states require disclosure of the initial board of directors and a business purpose, although there are interesting anonymity provisions in the laws of a few states. The person who signs the Articles can merely be the "incorporator," who does not have to be connected with the entity and who will have no authority relating to the entity thereafter, unless she is also a shareholder, director, or officer. In selecting the address and divulging other information in the Articles, consider your own anonymity. Do you really want the world to know where you live? Think about using a commercial mailing address, either your company's or a commercial mailbox facility.

In addition to state law filing, once the corporation is formed, there are tax issues to be dealt with. In order for the corporation to carry on its business, it needs to have a tax identification number for entities that is the employer identification number, or "EIN" for short. For federal income tax purposes, the corporation is a separate taxpayer, apart from its shareholders.

Different tax rules apply to corporations than to individuals, partnerships, trusts, and estates. These rules are set forth in Subchapter C of the Internal Revenue Code. A taxable corporation is properly referred to as a "C corporation" for federal income tax purposes. The corporate income tax rates run up the brackets from 15%, and a corporation does not enjoy any special rates for capital gains taxes. Thus, a corporation in the top tax bracket for its taxable income level will pay that amount on its capital gains as well and not the current 20% more favorable rate enjoyed by individuals, partners, estates and trusts. Personal service corporations, which are formed by people providing services such as doctors, lawyers, accountants, and so forth, pay tax at the top rate as a flat rate.

Because the C corporation is a separate taxable person, the phrase "double taxation" is often associated with it. Income tax is paid at two levels. That phrase means less today under current law than it used to, but often extra taxes are paid in trying to get funds out of a C corporation. Shareholders receiving money or property from the corporation in the form of dividends will pay a tax on the dividends (in 2013 at favorable rates of 0%, 15% and 20% depending on the recipient individual's overall tax bracket), and the corporation cannot take a tax deduction for what it pays out in dividends, hence the notion of double taxation. Tax is paid at the corporate level and possibly again at the individual shareholder level.

There are "single taxation" ways to get funds from a C corporation, however, and some other favorable tax strategies make the C corporation a worthwhile tax and legal entity to utilize. For example, any salary, wage, or independent contractor payment made to a shareholder, or anyone else for that matter, is deductible to the corporation, provided that the payment is for a proper business purpose.[1] The payment is includable in the recipient's gross income for his tax purposes, but that's the single tax, not a double tax as with a dividend. Rents paid for use of real estate, furniture, equipment, art, etc. are also deductible by the corporation and are then taxed to the lessor.

We should ask the question of why it is necessary to remove money or other assets from the corporation. If the corporation is engaged in business, are there things that the

---

1 Consider certain golden parachute payments as not being deductible.

shareholder can use for business purposes which can stay in the corporation, be owned by the corporation, and merely be used by the shareholder/employee? Cars and equipment are good examples, and if business travel is associated with the enterprise, perhaps a condo or other type of residence in a frequently visited location would make business sense, rather than payment for endless hotel rooms. Of course, while C corporations do not pay favorable rates on capital gains taxes, C corporations can engage in tax-free like-kind exchanges of real estate, if another location is needed. And there is no limit on how long a C corporation must stay in business and hang on to its property.

In addition to the techniques mentioned above for taking money out of a corporation besides dividends, *i.e.,* rent and payment for services, the corporation can also set up a retirement plan for its employees. This strategy works especially well if it is a closely held corporation with very few employees (for example, a sole employee who is also the sole shareholder of the business). The corporation sets up the retirement plan (profit sharing plan or defined benefit plan, perhaps preferably, due to larger deduction capabilities) and then gets a tax deduction for contributions to the plan. The shareholder-employee is the beneficiary and will, upon retirement and withdrawal of funds from the plan, pay taxes on those amounts, but those taxes will be the only taxes paid on the funds, and the amount will be dependent on the individual's tax situation, not the corporation's. So, at the end of the corporate life, there are no funds left to be double-taxed to the shareholders. Clearly this creative approach would not work in every situation, but there are many circumstances in which it could work very well.

What else do you get from a corporation? The general rule is that a shareholder is not responsible for the debts of the corporation. The corporation is historically one of the first limited liability type entities. But, unlike LLCs in many states and limited partnership interests, a corporation's shareholders can easily lose their shareholdings to their personal creditor claims. A judgment creditor could satisfy his claim against you by seizing your portfolio holdings in publicly traded stocks and bonds or by taking your shares in your closely held corporation.

Corporations are governed by the contents of their Articles of Incorporation, their Bylaws, and by resolutions passed by their shareholders and Board of Directors. The shareholders elect the Board of Directors, and the Directors then choose the officers of the corporation. The normal title for the chief executive officer of a corporation is president. Other officers can include a vice president, secretary, and treasurer, and various assistants to those roles can be selected for larger organizations. All officers answer to the Board of Directors. The president usually has broad powers for running the business of the corporation. Her backup or successor is the vice president if one is selected. The secretary is generally responsible for keeping corporate records such as minutes, resolutions, the bylaws, stock records, etc., and where required, attests to the correctness of the president's signature. Generally the president and the secretary sign stock certificates, when certificates are issued. The treasurer handles the finances and accounting for the corporation. In many states, one person can fill all of these officer positions.

Corporations seem to have waned in popularity as a legal entity of choice, at least in several parts of the country, with the advent of the limited liability company. There are many uses for them, nevertheless. Publicly traded companies are most often corporations, and the corporate format is a requirement for the companies trading on the various stock exchanges. Some states require that certain licenses be held solely in corporate format. For example, a limited liability company cannot hold a contractor's license in the state of California, which requires that the entity must be a corporation.

For the closely held business, the corporation may not be the best choice of entity, but it is important to consider its use when setting up a new enterprise.

While you are at it, don't forget to safeguard your business interests in the event of a divorce. Prenuptial and postnuptial agreements can work well in addition to holding the business in an irrevocable Trust. *See* Chapter 20.

27 WHAT TO DO ABOUT YOUR S CORP. IN YOUR ESTATE PLAN?

The S Corporation ("S corp.")[1] refers to a special federal tax election to have the corporation be taxed as a "flow-through" entity, rather than the entity itself being taxed, so that the shareholders proportionately report the taxable income of the corporation on their individual income tax returns and proportionately pay the taxes for the corporation. An LLC choosing to be taxed as a corporation can also make the S election, and as such, is referred to frequently as an LLC-S corp.

There are special rules about who can be a shareholder in an S corp. (or a member of an LLC-S corp.), and those rules generally limit shareholders to being individual U.S. citizens and resident aliens. Only special types of entities can

---

1 The S refers to Subchapter S of the Code, and the entity used to be officially referred to as a Subchapter S Corporation. That name has been simplified for a number of years. A corporation which has not made the S election is governed under Subchapter C of the Code and hence, is referred to as a C Corporation, meaning it is a stand-alone taxable entity.

be shareholders, as discussed below. Because of the usual desire to retain the flow-through tax treatment, death of a shareholder (which term will include a member of an LLC-S corp. for this discussion) can require treatment of S corp. shares in the estate plans of the shareholders.

A person's estate can be an S corp. shareholder for an unlimited period of time; however, estates cannot remain open forever, so practically, there is a time limit. A grantor trust is a qualified shareholder during the grantor's life time, and a testamentary trust can be an S corp. shareholder for two years. So, if the decedent has children or other heirs whom he wants to inherit the S corp. shares, those shares can be left outright to the children provided they are qualifying individuals (U.S. citizens or resident aliens).

Where minor children are involved or if there is the desire to hold the shares in trust for older beneficiaries for an extended period of time, there are two types of trusts which are specially designed to be qualified S corp. shareholders.

The Qualified Subchapter S Trust ("QSST") can only have one beneficiary who must receive by distribution all income for the S corp. shares owned by the trust each year and who must report the income on his individual tax return. A separate QSST must be set up for each inheriting beneficiary. Principal can be withheld, depending on the terms of the trust. The beneficiary must be a qualifying S corp. shareholder, that is, a citizen or resident alien of the U.S. The QSST can also be a Qualified Terminable Property Interest ("QTIP") trust for a spouse.[2]

The second qualified S corp. shareholder trust is known as an Electing Small Business Trust ("ESBT"). It can have

---

2 A QTIP Trust, established under Code Sec. 2056, allows a 100% marital deduction against estate taxes for assets passing to it yet provides that the Trustor can control the distribution rights of beneficiaries to the trust estate once the spouse as beneficiary has died. See Chapter 8 for additional discussion.

multiple beneficiaries and hold or distribute income. Distributed income is taxed to the beneficiaries or if held, it is taxable to the trust. Distributed or held income, however, is taxed at the highest individual tax bracket on ordinary income. Beneficiaries can include charitable organizations and estates.

There are a number of reasons for choosing an outright distribution, a QSST, or an ESBT for your heirs. It will be important for the S corp. shareholder to identify his desires regarding the disposition of company ownership through stock distributions so that his Will or trust will contain the correct determination.

One of the rules about an S corp. is that it can only have one class of stock, that is, common stock, not preferred. Common stock may, however, be divided between voting and nonvoting shares, so long as both types of shares have the same distribution and liquidation rights. Where there is a desire to give control to one person but to share equity among several, the revision of the corporate governing documents to create the two types of common stock, voting and nonvoting, can be useful.

Tom's Story. Tom founded a very successful company many years ago, and as he became older, he put one of his sons, Bill, in charge of operations. Bill has successfully guided the company and helped it grow, and now that Tom is in his 70s, he wants to be sure that Bill can stay in control and not be removed by his siblings, who also own shares. Ten years ago, Tom gave away 40% of the stock in varying proportions to his six children. He is now looking for a plan to continue to benefit the whole family with his remaining 60% but still leave Bill in control. The following plan was submitted to the seven shareholders and unanimously approved. The Articles of Incorporation were amended to split the stock into 10% voting shares and 90% nonvoting shares. Forty percent of the nonvoting shares represent the shares already held by the six children. Tom will give and sell his nonvoting shares, representing 50% equity to an intentionally defective grantor trust ("IDGT") taking back a self-canceling installment note ("SCIN") for the purchase price. The IDGT will provide for immediate distribution of the shares at Tom's death to the children as beneficiaries. His estate planning documents have been written to provide that his remaining 10% of the stock, which constitutes all of the voting stock in the company, will be split 60% to Bill, so he stays in charge, and 40% to his daughter Melissa who has been serving on the Board of Directors. The 10% voting stock will be included in his estate for estate tax purposes. The company can continue to be taxed as an S corp. because all of the individual shareholders are US citizens, and Tom's shares are held in his revocable living trust and in the IDGT, both of which are grantor trusts, during his lifetime.

While there were several issues to be resolved in planning Tom's estate in the example above, it was very important that his major asset, the S corp., be identified and specifically addressed.

28 BUYING AND SELLING A BUSINESS

"I'm ready to sell my business."—All business owners have days when they mutter something along these lines. But, what does it actually mean to "sell my business"? Suppose you have a willing buyer who has tentatively agreed to pay a certain purchase price. What is next?

The first question that typically arises is whether the buyer is going to purchase the entire entity (*i.e.*, corporation, limited liability company, or partnership) or all or just some of the assets of the entity? From the buyer's perspective, a purchase of the entire entity is less attractive since it means not only buying all of the assets owned by the entity, but also acquiring all of the entity's liabilities, known and unknown. There are factors that might motivate a buyer to purchase the entire entity, such as a desire to avoid issues related to the assignment of critical contracts, licenses, or identification numbers (*e.g.,* standard unique health identifiers for health care providers). But, for the most part, a buyer will usually elect an asset purchase, which enables the buyer to buy less than all the assets and allows the buyer to pick and choose which liabilities, if any, to assume.

The second question that needs to be addressed is what are the tax implications of the proposed transaction? If the entire entity is being sold, then the seller will typically owe taxes on her gains at the capital gains rate on the difference between the purchase price the buyer is paying and the seller's tax basis in the entity. So, for a simple example, if the seller's tax basis is $40,000 and the buyer pays $100,000 for 100% ownership of the entity, the seller will be taxed on the gain of $60,000, usually and mostly at favorable capital gain rates.

With an asset sale, the tax implications are more complex. Basically, the purchase price is allocated among the assets individually, based on the fair market value of each asset, as agreed upon by the buyer and seller. The buyer and seller must agree upon such allocation, and both parties must report identical information to the IRS. The issue of how to allocate the purchase price is often a sticking point when it comes to an asset sale, since how the assets are valued has different tax ramifications for the buyer and the seller.

For instance, you might think that a "customer list" is only as valuable as the "goodwill" associated with the seller. However, the portion of the purchase price allocated to the seller's "customer list" will be taxed as ordinary income, meaning it will be taxed at the seller's marginal tax rate (normally 28% to 39.6%) while the portion of the purchase price allocated to "goodwill" will be taxed as long term capital gains, provided the seller has owned the business for more than a year. If the seller provides a "covenant not to compete" to the buyer, any portion of the purchase price allocated to it will be taxed as ordinary income. From the buyer's perspective, however, there is no difference in the tax treatment of the portion of the purchase price allocated to the seller's "customer list" versus the seller's "goodwill" versus the seller's "non-compete." All of the amounts, allocated to those items must be amortized, or deducted evenly, over 15 years by the buyer. Understanding the tax treatment of the various components of the purchased price can be valuable in the negotiations.

Getting the buyer and the seller to agree upon a price allocation can be one of the most challenging issues related to the sale of a business. For instance, the buyer will want it to be clear that the seller is receiving something as consideration for the promise not to compete. Otherwise, the seller might argue that such covenant is nothing more than an unenforceable "gratuitous promise." One way to achieve a "win-win" situation is, rather than allocating a certain dollar amount, to have the asset sale contract specifically spell out that the consideration for the non-compete is the mutual promises of the parties and other provisions contained within the agreement. Often, the key to resolving any disputes over the allocation of the purchase price is to think creatively when structuring the deal.

Whether or not you wind up selling the entire entity or just some or all of its assets, there are several things to do prior to offering the business to prospective buyers in order to improve the odds of a successful transaction. First and foremost, your entity and accounting books must be in order, with clear, easily understood financials ready to be inspected by a prospective buyer. A good buyer will engage in due diligence to be sure that what is being purchased is a viable, real business. Only your books and tax returns can verify the truth behind your representations as seller. You need to know your numbers inside and out, so it is important to hire an accountant who is not only experienced with buying and selling businesses, but who can crunch your numbers and explain them to both of you in layperson's terms. Be ready to explain your annual profit margin, recent developments affecting the business, and what a new owner should expect as far as required time, effort, and capital investment in order to continue running the business successfully.

Frank's Story. Frank decided it was time to retire and sell his handyman business. He figured he could get $500,000 for it, since he had been taking $100,000 a year out of it as profit, and someone told him a 20% return per year was a good return on investment. Frank had never used an accountant. Why should he when it was easy to use a computer program for preparing his tax returns and pay his taxes on the $100,000 a year he took out? A friend who is a business broker agreed to list the business for him, but told him he probably could not get $500,000 for it. A large company fairly soon came along but after seeing that Frank's accounting was only done in his check register and that he only had simple tax returns for the business, quickly backed away. Frank then hired an accountant who helped him put together some better financial statements, reassess what he had to sell, and arrive at a better listing price. Within a short period of time, Frank got a buyer for cash, sold his business at a more desired price, and is now enjoying his retirement!

Before you share any sensitive information with a prospective buyer, it is imperative that you have him sign a "non-disclosure and non-use" agreement. The "non-use" element is one that is often missed with a standard non-disclosure agreement ("NDA"). A promise not to disclose a secret does not necessarily mean a promise not to use such information, so you have to cover both contingencies. There are other elements of an effective NDA that necessitate the input of a good attorney, so be sure to find one early on.

Another reason it is important to consult with an experienced business attorney before you offer your business for sale is to ensure that you do not inadvertently run afoul of any state or federal securities laws. While it is legal to publicly offer to sell 100% of your business, if you offer to sell any amount less than 100%, you may then offering to sell securities. And, generally speaking, if you are offering to sell securities without either (a) properly registering the offering as an initial public offering (an "IPO"), or (b) complying with the federal and state requirements of an unregistered private offering, lots of bad things can happen, especially if you are making such an offer online or through other advertising or otherwise to the public at large. In addition to keeping you out of hot water, a knowledgeable business lawyer can also make sure the entity's internal documentation is all in order, including, for an asset sale, a duly-executed resolution authorizing the company to offer Its assets for sale.

Depending on the type of business, you may want to use the services of a local "business broker" to help market your business and identify and screen prospective buyers. However, it is important to keep in mind that, depending on what state you live in, business brokers are not required to be licensed attorneys. Often, business brokers are not well regulated and the services they provide arguably amount to the practice of law without a license. In some states, such as Arizona, anybody with a (residential) real estate license can hold themselves out as a commercial business broker. Because it can be expensive to hire a business broker (they typically get a commission of 10% to 30% or more), you may be tempted to use the "standard form" documents offered by the business broker. However, this is one area where an ounce of prevention can be worth a ton of cure. No two deals are ever the same, and the services of a good contract-drafting attorney with tax knowledge are going to be well worth the additional expense. By being able to creatively structure the sale of your business, you can realize tremendous tax savings while avoiding misunderstandings between you and the buyer that can lead to very expensive legal disputes. Selling a business is not like selling a car or even a house;

you will almost certainly have an ongoing relationship with the buyer at least for a while, usually to train the buyer or simply by being available for post-closing consultation to facilitate a smooth transition. Often, the seller is formally hired by the buyer, as either an employee or a consultant, to continue running the company until the buyer is ready to take it over completely (or can train someone else to do so). So, paying to have a well-drafted, easily understood purchase and sale agreement, with related documents (*e.g.,* post-closing employment or consultation agreement), is going to be money well spent. And if you still need a business broker to help market your business, your local business attorney is sure to know a few good ones.

There are many questions to consider when selling your company: how to structure the deal, how to protect your sensitive information, how to avoid committing securities law Infractions, how to minimize your taxes, and how to help the buyer be successful post-closing. The best way to avoid these worrying questions is to hire capable professionals to help you, starting with a skilled business attorney and an experienced accountant.

29 RETIREMENT PLANNING

From a tax planning, savings, investment, and asset protection standpoint, retirement plans of various sorts deserve serious consideration. Many of us think that we have to rely entirely on employers to set up plans, and many employers, often being small business owners themselves, do not provide anything for their employees. Even if a person does not receive retirement plan benefits through employment, there are tax-advantaged ways in which each person can put away funds for retirement and enjoy some asset protection. Whole books are written on the various retirement plans, so this chapter is intended to provide a summary of some types of plans and ideas of how they can be effectively used, not only for retirement funding but also for current tax planning.

A defined contribution plan (such as a profit sharing plan) and a defined benefit plan are types of retirement plans which are governed by select provisions of the Internal Revenue Code and the Employee Retirement Income Security Act ("ERISA"). These are often referred to as "qualified" plans, which means they meet the requirements of the Code and ERISA provisions. Qualified plans can generally be established by any type of company having at least one employee who receives taxable wages subject to employment taxes. C corporations, S corporations, partnerships, and sole proprietorships (and the LLC versions of those entities) may have qualified plans.

A defined benefit plan promises the participant a specific monthly benefit, *i.e.*, a dollar amount, at retirement. Monthly benefits are calculated through a formula that considers a participant's salary and length of service, meaning how long he has been employed. A formula might include something fairly standard such as a lifetime pension payable monthly, beginning at a set retirement age (such as 65) of an annual percentage of the final average compensation times the years of counted employment (reduced if less than 10 years of service). An actuary must calculate the minimum and maximum amounts an employer must contribute each year to the plan in order to meet the employer's future obligation to employees who retire under the plan. Such projections are completed on the basis of actuarial assumptions, computations, and plan provisions. Generally, the contribution amounts are greater for older employees than younger employees since there is less time to accumulate the projected defined benefit at an older employee's retirement.

Under a defined contribution plan, the emphasis is on the contribution to the plan at the time it is made rather than on how much benefit the contribution yields at the retirement age of the employee. There are several types of defined contribution plans, including a money purchase pension plan, which requires an annual contribution by the employer, and a profit sharing plan, under which the employer makes contributions on a discretionary basis. Other types of defined contribution plans include 401(k) plans and employee stock ownership plans ("ESOPs"). What a participant in a defined contribution plan ultimately receives will depend upon the amount contributed to the plan for her benefit over the period of her employment and the performance of the investment of plan assets over the period until she retires.

A qualified retirement plan provides significant current tax benefits by allowing an employer to claim a deduction for contributions to a qualified retirement plan while permitting the deferral of taxation on the related income of the participants until a later year, such as a year in which a distribution from the plan occurs (typically upon retirement).

In addition to deductions for the employer who makes contributions, any employee contributions (primarily found in defined contribution plans) are not subject to current income tax, although employment taxes are still assessed against those earnings. It helps the employee's tax planning to be able to make these pre-tax contributions.

Subject to certain rules, a qualified plan is itself a tax-exempt entity. That means that the plan pays no tax on its receipt of contributions from the sponsoring employer, and further that earnings on plan investments, such as interest, dividends, and capital gains, are tax-free. That allows plan assets not reduced by any tax payments to grow at a rate of 100 cents on the dollar.

The Code and ERISA contain a complex set of rules (accompanied by an equally complex set of Regulations issued respectively by the Department of Treasury and the Department of Labor) that govern qualified retirement plans, and specify the means by which a plan is "qualified." Rules include restrictions on discrimination against employees, investments that can be made, and pay-out requirements.

Absent the meeting of such qualifications, the plan's current tax benefits as described above are generally lost to the employer and to the plan.

Despite the many steps required for compliance, the benefits to an employer as well as to its employees can be significant and add to the quality of the work force and production. For a small employer with an owner who works in the business or a sole proprietor, the profit sharing and defined benefit plans can create significant current tax savings, provide a means to grow retirement savings on a tax-free basis, and insure an income stream once retirement age is reached.

Don't forget your Individual Retirement Account ("IRA"). The IRA is a tax-favored way to set up a savings account for yourself, to use the funds when you retire. You can make contributions to a traditional IRA, in which you get a current income tax deduction, or to a Roth IRA which can provide tax-free retirement benefits. The 2013 contribution limit for both a traditional IRA and a Roth IRA is the lesser of your taxable compensation or $5500 per person ($6500 if you are over age 50) per year.[1] You cannot contribute to a traditional IRA after you reach age 70 ½, but there is no age limit on rollovers from other plans to IRAs and on making Roth IRA contributions.

You may want to roll over funds from your employer's funds when you leave that job into your IRA or perhaps you have had a qualified plan in your own company that is now inactive. Rolling your benefits into your IRA keeps the funds tax-free, allowing for 100% growth before taxes. You are only taxed when you take out the funds.

Many people are stymied by the 10% penalty rule concerning IRAs (which penalty also applies to all qualified

---

1 *See* www.IRS.gov for each year's contribution limits.

retirement plans and tax-deferred annuities). The general rule is that if you withdraw any amount from the IRA before reaching age 59 ½, you are subject to a 10% penalty on the IRA funds in addition to the usual income taxation. That means if you withdraw $20,000 from your IRA at age 55, you will include the $20,000 on your personal income tax return as an ordinary income item, thereby increasing your taxable income potentially by the $20,000, and you will pay an extra $2,000 in tax for the 10% penalty.

There are, however, exceptions to this seemingly harsh rule. If you become disabled, which is defined in the Code as being unable to engage in substantial gainful activity which condition is expected to be of long duration,[2] then you may withdraw your IRA funds without the 10% penalty regardless of your age. The IRS will not give you a ruling on your disability, so it is up to you as the taxpayer to document your disability with doctor's reports, etc.

There are other hardship exceptions, as well, including needing payments for medical care; purchasing a principal residence; tuition for self, spouse, children and other dependents; payments to prevent eviction from the principal residence; funeral expenses for yourself, spouse, children and dependents; and certain expenses to repair damage to your principal residence.

Melinda's Story. Melinda at age 52 had a lot of investments which were presently illiquid, and she was having difficulty paying for her home, her car, child's expenses, business debts, and medical expenses. She withdrew $200,000 from her IRA to use for her needs. A couple of months after the withdrawal, she found her situation so depressing, however, that she pulled her older Bentley automobile into her garage, shut the garage door with the car running, and intentionally died of carbon monoxide poisoning. Her estate's executor was able

---

2 IRC Sec. 72(m)(7); Treas. Regs. Sec. 1.72-17A(f)(1); and IRC Sec. 72(t)(2)(1)(A)(iii).

to claim her illness as a disability and avoid the extra $20,000 of income tax which would have been levied under the 10% penalty rule but for the hardship exception.

Another exception is that you may choose to take out your IRA funds prior to reaching age 59 ½ if you take the funds out in equal periodic payments over a period of time based on your life expectancy. If you are 55, have a life expectancy of at least 30 more years, and have $100,000 in your IRA, you may remove $3333 per year from the IRA for the remainder of your life, without the 10% penalty.[3] The good news is that even with this payment plan, at age 59 you can change the distribution plan without the 10% penalty.

You may be disenchanted with your current IRA custodian. There are many IRA custodians to choose from; every bank and brokerage company as well as credit unions can serve as custodian and offer IRA investment opportunities. An IRA-to-IRA rollover, in which you change custodians and move the funds directly from one account to the other without you taking any possession of the funds, is income tax and penalty free.

You may also pull the funds out of your IRA taking personal possession of them. In that situation, your IRA custodian must withhold 20% of your withdrawal for income taxes. You then have sixty (60) days in which to re-deposit those funds into the old IRA or into a new IRA to avoid income taxation or the 10% penalty, if applicable. At that point, however, you only have 80% of the IRA withdrawal in your possession, so to avoid the tax and penalty on the 20% withdrawal, you must also re-deposit the 20% withheld tax amount, which you will need to provide from other sources. When you file your income tax return for the year, if you have overpaid taxes due to the 20% withholding on your original IRA withdrawal, you should receive a refund of the 20% at that time.

---

3 IRC Sec. 72(t)(2)(A)(iv).

When you have a Roth IRA, which is a special IRA that gives you no tax deduction for funds going in but which grows tax free and enables you to withdraw funds on a tax-free basis, there is no limit on how long your Roth can last before you withdraw the funds. With a traditional IRA, however, while you get a tax deduction for qualifying contributions and have tax-free growth, you will be taxed on every dollar you withdraw, and you must begin withdrawing the IRA funds when you reach 70 ½. Your withdrawal must be made by April 1 of the calendar year following your 70 ½ date.

That date, April 1 of the calendar year following the year when you reach 70 ½, is referred to as the Required Beginning Date. While you can take all of your IRA contributions out on your Required Beginning Date, that's not usually a good idea. Remember that your IRA withdrawals are subject to income tax. You are allowed to "stretch" your withdrawals out over your life expectancy. Your Required Minimum Distribution ("RMD") in any given year is the balance of your IRA and other pension funds divided by the number of years you are actuarially determined to continue to live. If you have $100,000 in your traditional IRA and a life expectancy of 14 years, based on tables published by the Department of Treasury, then your RMD for that year is $100,000 divided by 14 or $7,143.00. You can recalculate your RMD every year. If you have multiple IRAs, you must combine them to determine the RMD for each year, but you can take your entire RMD out of one plan. You can do the same thing for pension plans (they have to be counted in the overall amount of retirement funds you have to calculate RMD) but you cannot take the pension portion out of the IRA and vice versa.

A good estate planning tool for your pension plans and traditional IRAs is to make your charitable contributions out of the taxable pension and IRA funds. If you leave those funds directly to your family and other heirs as beneficiaries, they will pay income tax on those funds. The funds are referred to as "income in respect of a decedent" ("IRD") which basically means that they will pay the taxes on the funds that you did not pay. Remember that Roth IRA funds are not subject to this income tax because you have not taken tax deductions for amounts contributed to the Roth IRA. If you plan to make a charitable contribution at your death, then designation of the charities as beneficiaries of the IRA funds avoids that income tax. Charities are, by their nature, income tax free, so the charities will not recognize any IRD income. Your other assets which will pass income tax free to all heirs may be used for the distributions to your children and other beneficiaries.

30 PLANNING FOR YOUR OWN CARE AT ANY AGE

We have all heard the stories about the aged parent who was doing well on her own until she took a fall and broke a hip. But what about the fifty-four year old who develops early on-set Alzheimer's Disease and by age fifty-eight needs round-the-clock care? In this country, medical needs are paid for through Medicare for the elderly, health insurance, private pay, and Medicaid and similar programs for the impoverished. Other than limited care plans for those on Medicare who are recuperating (a little over 3 months maximum) or persons qualifying at the poverty level, there is no national governmental system to pay for long-term care except each person's private funds. The new national health care acts[1] have not made a change in long-term care provisions.

In addition to the issue of how to pay

---

1 The Patient Protection and Affordable Care Act (March 23, 2010) and The Health Care and Education Reconciliation Act of 2010 (March 30, 2010).

for such care, most people, including the vulnerable elderly, have not given thought to where they would want to be cared for. It is a classic case of denial or refusing to admit that such a circumstance could happen to them.

Nursing home costs across the country range from $3,000 per month to much higher depending on a person's needs. Small group homes can be somewhat less expensive. In-home care by qualified professionals can range from $15-75 per hour, based again on the type of care is needed.

There is often the need to protect the assets of the healthy spouse so she will not later be financially impaired because all of the money was spent caring for the ill spouse.

Long-term care insurance may be available, provided that the person is insurable. The test for insurability can be different for this kind of insurance than for life insurance. The types of coverage are numerous, so a study of what each policy provides is useful in choosing the right policy to acquire. Annual premiums will vary depending on the coverage selected, the age of the insured when the policy is issued, and the company. An average annual premium for a healthy person in her fifties is $2500. This may seem like a high premium amount, but if and when the coverage is needed, that premium amount is less than even one month in a care facility. Further, the premium amount cannot be raised because of an individual's situation but rather must be raised for all insureds across the board, if the company is experiencing overall higher costs and gets permission from the state's insurance department for a blanket increase.

Coverage can include payment of a specific dollar per day, a percentage of the costs (60-80%), in-home care as well as care at a facility, limited term or life-time care, etc. Policies can also have life insurance components and refund provisions built in. Even people who believe they can comfortably self-pay will often acquire the long-term care policy coverage in order to limit their risks.

Usually the decision for long-term care must be made quickly, in an emergency situation. Prior planning, for payment, as well as choices of location or type of facility can save a family and the individual needing care a great deal of time and avoid emotional stress. *See* Chapter 31 for a fuller discussion of elder care issues.

Hilda's Story. The 85-year old woman, Hilda, developed colon cancer, and throughout all of her chemo and radiation treatment, she was able to live at home with her aged yellow Labrador. She made a Will but refused to sign a power of attorney or health care power of attorney because she did not want anyone else to have any authority over her, and certainly not her brother and sister or their ungrateful children. Her attorney did get her to express her wishes regarding end of life treatment in a living will and to set forth her desires for cremation. Otherwise, she was on her own, caring for herself and dog at home, and not being interfered with. Then one day, her neighbor visited and immediately called the ambulance because the neighbor found Hilda in bad shape, unable to get out of bed, feed the dog, or clean herself. She never returned home. The dog was taken to the vet for care. After the hospital, she wound up in a care facility with only marginally competent staff. They left her alone for hours, hurt her when turning her, did not bathe her regularly, and seemed to be overdosing her with meds. She had no one she could talk to about it as even her telephone access was limited. Finally, she was able to scribble a note on a scrap of paper to her attorney and have another patient's family member mail it for her. The scrawled writing said simply, "Get me out of here!" It took the attorney a week to locate her before she could be moved to a better location.

Even though Hilda generally had her mental faculties and could make her own decisions, she lapsed due to her health. Powers of attorney would have enabled someone else to make inquiries about her, review her medical condition, and get her into a better facility much sooner. She also could have visited various care facilities in her area of the city and made known where she wanted to go, if the need arose. Fortunately, she had an attorney she could call on, although it had been three years since she had had any contact with him.

Hilda did not clearly understand the importance of personal planning. None of us can predict what our future needs or circumstances might be. She did not know what she did not know. Planning for your later care is a must. Do not leave the decisions for someone else to make for you.

Gertrude's Story. Gertrude was widowed at age 84. She and her husband had four children, who as adults were doing well. They all lived in the same town as she, and while the three sons left a great deal in their sister's hands when it came to Mom, they were all duly attentive. Gertrude lived in the large ranch house where all of the children had grown up and where she now entertained hoards of grandchildren and great grandchildren. At age 90, however, Gertrude had had enough of the big house. She asked her daughter to take her to three independent living apartment-style facilities. The daughter was aghast but decided to do what Mom wanted. Gertrude liked one of them, signed up on the 2-month wait list on the spot, and went home, contacted a realtor and put the big house on the market. The children and grandchildren gathered around to try to talk her out of it, but Gertrude explained that she was tired, wanted something new, and did not want any of them having to care for her. Gertrude got busy. She hired a helper to assist her in going through her belongings. She distributed her heirlooms to all who wanted them, had a garage sale, and donated the rest to charity. When the house sold soon, she was ready and the apartment was ready, and she moved. She loved it there: she played bridge and Canasta, took the facility's shuttle to go shopping, ate lunch and dinner with new people, and felt secure in her private apartment. After a few years at that facility, Gertrude knew it was time for a higher level of care. She again asked her daughter to take her around to some places offering assisted living, and made her choice and moved. She felt more secure and had nursing assistance when she needed it. When Gertrude passed away at age 99, she was surrounded by her entire family and left them the legacy of how to plan for one's own care needs.

31 ELDER LAW
By Marsha Goodman, Esq.

Elder Law is a relatively new area of the law which recognizes that individuals face special legal challenges as they grow older. It is defined not so much by the type of transactions that are included, as it is by the concerns of aging adults and their family members. For example, every adult should have a general power of attorney, health care power of attorney and living will, for all the reasons described in Chapter 5. But for older adults, the need may be much more immediate, and the person they would most like to serve as their agent may no longer be living. There may also be issues of the individual's competence to give the authority or the potential exploitation by someone who is motivated by his own self-interest.

Diminished Capacity

When we talk about a person's competence to give his authority through a power of attorney or sign a legal document, we are really referring to the idea of diminished capacity. While most of us will not suffer diminished capacity to make decisions, the risk of Alzheimer's Disease and other dementias does increase as we age, and some people clearly lose the ability to make informed decisions about their assets or their care. But what about the person who is occasionally forgetful, or who has just been diagnosed with Mild Cognitive Impairment? Does this make that person immediately incapable of expressing an informed opinion?

The determination of whether someone lacks legal capacity is not a medical decision, but a legal one. Some legal documents give a doctor the authority to make that decision, but the physician's opinion only determines the person's capacity because the legal document says that it does. For example, a trust may say that the trustor may be removed as his own trustee when two physicians say that he is no longer legally competent to make decisions regarding his finances, or a power of attorney may say that the agent's authority becomes effective when the principal's primary care physician says that she can no longer make responsible decisions about her own care. Similarly, although the report of a physician may carry great weight, a court, and not that physician, decides whether someone is so incapacitated that he needs to have a guardian appointed to make his healthcare decisions or a conservator appointed to manage his financial affairs.

There are different definitions of capacity for different types of legal transactions. Testamentary capacity (the capacity to prepare a Will) is a relatively low standard, whereas the capacity to enter into a complex contract with lots of legal boilerplate is a much higher one. A person will be considered to have testamentary capacity if he has a general understanding of the nature and extent of his property (for example, he knows he owns a home and some stock, and has a couple of bank accounts, but not necessarily the name of the brokerage house or the balances of those accounts) and can propose a rational plan for disposing of them (for example, "I want my son to make the arrangements to give my house to the daughter who has been living with me to take care of me, and everything else divided between my grandchildren"). Similarly, some states recognize that someone has the capacity to sign a power of attorney if she has a basic understanding that she wants her oldest daughter to help pay her bills or manage her bank account, even if she doesn't understand the term "power of attorney." And the person must only have legal capacity at the time the Will is signed. It does not matter if he lacked capacity before the signing (for example, due to an illness), or if he is not able to remember the execution or existence of the Will shortly thereafter.

Individuals who sign documents as witnesses are confirming that, in their opinion, the signer had sufficient capacity to sign the document at the time of signing. Signers who are concerned that someone may attack a document in the future may consider having an attorney question them on videotape, as a way to document that they had a clear understanding of the purpose of the document and the meaning of its terms at the time that they signed it.

Some elders are victimized by unscrupulous people who take advantage of their diminished capacity. State laws designed to protect seniors and punish the perpetrators use the term "vulnerable adult," defined as someone over age 18 who is unable to protect herself from abuse or exploitation because of a physical or mental impairment. This would include someone who might be victimized by a person who presents himself as knowledgeable or helpful for the purpose of taking advantage of the senior's confusion about technology or banking requirements. These laws protect vulnerable adults who are much less incapacitated than someone who requires a conservator to manage her affairs. However, the mere diagnosis of certain progressive conditions, such as

Mild Cognitive Impairment or Parkinson's Disease, does not automatically mean that the person's capacity has diminished to the point that he is legally vulnerable. Again, the courts would consider all of the facts, only one of which is that person's diagnosis.

Long-Term Care

The event that causes most people to seek an elder law attorney is the realization that they or a loved one requires long-term care. This may be the result of a catastrophic incident, such as a fall or a stroke, or the gradual decline of a person who has been living independently, such that she is no longer safe at home alone.

Medicare

When a senior suffers a catastrophic incident, if she has established her eligibility, Medicare Part A covers the cost of the initial hospitalization, subject to certain deductibles and co-pays which change every year. The publication "Medicare and You," which is prepared each year by the Centers for Medicare and Medicaid and is available at all Social Security Offices and online at www.Medicare.gov provides an excellent overview of these fees, as well as a description of the services that are covered by Medicare.

More and more, hospitals provide only the most acute care, with any rehabilitation being delivered in separate, skilled nursing facilities. Medicare will cover up to 100 days in an acute care setting, which can be in a hospital, a Skilled Nursing Facility ("SNF"), or a combination of the two, as long the individual was admitted to the hospital for up to 3 days at the beginning of the period. While the patient is generally discharged from the hospital to the SNF, the time in the SNF will be covered if the patient is admitted to the SNF within 30 days of discharge from the hospital. If the patient is discharged from the SNF, and then admitted back to the hospital, for either the same or a different reason, within 6 months of the date of discharge, the cost of hospitalization or care in the SNF will only be covered if the total number of days is no more than 100. The patient must not receive care in a hospital or SNF for at least 6 months to start a new "benefit period," and therefore a new 100-day clock.

Medicare covers 100% of the cost of the SNF for the first 20 days. For 80 days after that, Medicare covers 80% of the cost. If the patient has a supplemental insurance policy, that policy will cover all or part of the remaining 20%; if not, the patient is personally responsible for that co-pay. Once Medicare will no longer cover Skilled Nursing Care, either because they've decided it's not medically feasible or necessary, or the 100 days has run out, a supplemental policy won't cover it, either.

For seriously ill patients, Medicare covers up to 80% of the cost of an additional 60 days of acute care. This is a lifetime allowance, so once the additional 60 days have been used, they are no longer available, even after a separate hospitalization.

What Medicare Doesn't Cover

Basically, Medicare does not cover custodial care. In order for a person to remain in an acute-care rehabilitation facility, he must be able to withstand 3 hours of rehabilitation therapy a day. If he is not strong enough to participate in this much therapy, or if he is simply not motivated to do so, then the care is simply custodial, and is not covered by Medicare.

Historically, Medicare, and the facilities that have been paid by Medicare, have also discontinued coverage of a person who was no longer showing improvement following therapy. For example, if a person reached a plateau following a stroke so that she could transfer from the bed to the wheelchair but could not regain the ability to walk, the facility would determine that further therapy was no longer medically necessary and the patient would be discharged. However, a recent court decision has confirmed the correct standard, which is whether the person continues to need the therapy in order to maintain her condition. For example, if the patient described above would lose the ability to transfer from the bed to the wheelchair if her therapy were discontinued, then she should not be discharged.

Regardless of the standard, however, the amount of coverage that Medicare will provide for inpatient care or therapy is limited to the time periods summarized above.

Medicare does not cover the cost of non- acute or "custodial care," such as non-medical home care, independent or assisted living, or even residence in a memory care unit for people suffering from dementia due to a stroke, Alzheimer's or other cause. Individuals who do not have the means to pay for this care must look to other sources of funding.

Medicaid

The funding source that most individuals look to for custodial care is Medicaid. The program may go by a different name in your state (such as The Arizona Health Care Cost Containment System (AHCCCS) in Arizona, or Medi-Cal in California), as each state is permitted to establish its own program. However, all programs must follow specific guidelines established by the federal government. The discussion below is specifically based on Arizona's implementation of the Medicaid program and it is a reasonable sample of how the various states interpret the federal rules.

The aspect of Medicaid that has been in the news lately relates to health insurance coverage for low income individuals and families. This portion is not relevant to most seniors, since they receive their health insurance coverage through Medicare. The aspect of Medicaid that is applicable to most seniors is that portion which pays for assisted living or skilled nursing care, the "custodial care" that Medicare does not cover for disabled adults and those over the age of 65.

In order for one's care to be covered by Medicaid, he must meet both a medical and a financial test. The medical standard is that, due to dementia and/or a physical condition, the person requires "nursing home level care." The evaluation is conducted by a medical evaluator (either a nurse or a social worker) employed by the Medicaid agency, who establishes a point score based on the person's ability to perform his activities of daily living. The standard is based on the need for care, even if the person is still living at home. However, the fact that the person resides in an assisted living facility does not necessarily affect the score that the evaluator will give. Medicaid eligibility may still be rejected. Families should be careful not to spend down their assets on the assumption that the senior will qualify for Medicaid if it is possible that he will not meet the medical standard.

The financial standard is a two-part test, which considers both income and asset value. In order to be eligible for Medicaid, the maximum amount of income that a single person can earn is $2,130 per month. (This is the figure for 2013, and it increases by the same Cost of Living Adjustment used to change Social Security benefits each year.) If the person is married, the agency will look first to the income that the applicant himself earns. This is called the "name on the check" rule, and means, for example, if the only income that the person applying for benefits earns is Social Security in the amount of one-half of her spouse's benefit amount, and that amount is less than $2,130, it does not matter how much income the spouse may earn in his own name. If, however, the income of the person who is applying for benefits is more than $2,130 per month, Medicaid will combine the income earned by both spouses. If half of that amount is no more than $2,130, then the person applying for benefits meets the income test.

Even if the person's income exceeds the maximum, it is possible for that person to meet the standard if he creates an Income-Only Trust.[1] This is a specific type of trust, the sole purpose of which is to enable someone with excess income to qualify for Medicaid, if he should find that his income is insufficient to cover the cost of residential care. The person identifies a source of some of his income (for example, a pension) which causes him to exceed the income standard, and opens a bank account in the name of the Income Only Trust into which that source of income will be direct-deposited. That income is the only source of funds for that account, and the funds must be used to contribute to the share of cost. The trust must specify that the funds cannot be used for any expenditures other than those that are allowed by the applicable regulations (including, for example, the share of cost and health insurance premiums and other medical expenses for the person on Medicaid), and the Medicaid has the first lien on any funds that might be remaining in the account upon the death of the person who has been receiving the Medicaid benefits.

The recipient of Medicaid benefits is not permitted to use his income as he wishes. Medicaid allows him to continue to cover the cost any health insurance, including Medicare Parts B and D, and he can keep a personal care allowance of about $100 per month. If the person is in a care facility, all income in excess of that amount is paid to the facility to cover the recipient's "share of cost." (There is no obligation to cover a share of the cost of Medicaid services provided in the person's home).

---

1 A few states do not have an income standard. In those states, anyone who meets the medical standard and the asset test is eligible for Medicaid, as long as they contribute the share of cost commensurate with their income. In those states, an Income-Only Trust would not be necessary.

If the recipient of Medicaid benefits is married, the law recognizes that it does not do that couple, let alone the state's social service agencies, any good to require the spouse to try to maintain her household if her income is less than the amount which Congress has determined is a livable wage ($1,892/month in 2013). In this case, before assessing the share of cost, the spouse who is not receiving care (referred to as the "community spouse" because she is still living in the community) can keep that portion of the institutionalized spouse's income necessary to bring her income up to this level, before the share of cost is assessed. She may be able to retain even more if there are additional dependents, or she can document that more is needed to maintain her home.

The standard with which most people are familiar is the asset standard. In order to be eligible for Medicaid, a single person may own assets worth no more than $2,000. This does not include the value of the person's primary residence or vehicle (even if she can no longer use them); their personal and household goods; burial plot and prepaid funeral, or an irrevocable insurance policy that would cover the cost of these items and services; and some additional exceptions related to income-generating property, such as rental properties or commercial equipment. Certain types of annuities, designed to be fully paid out during the recipient's lifetime, are also not counted as assets, although the payouts are counted as income. Real property that is not the primary residence or the source of income is considered a countable asset, as are checking and savings accounts, brokerage accounts and other financial investments, IRAs and 401(k)s, and the cash value of life insurance policies. These are referred to by Medicaid as "countable assets."

An applicant who is married to someone who is not also applying for Medicaid is known as the "Community Spouse." In addition to the $2,000 that the person applying for benefits is permitted to own, the Community Spouse is allowed to retain half of the couple's countable assets, up to a maximum of $115,920.[2] This is called the "Community Spouse Resource Assessment," or CSRA. When a married person applies for benefits, the Medicaid agency will review the financial information that the applicant provides, and advise him of the CSRA as of the date of the claim. Assuming the person meets the medical and income criteria, he will become eligible for benefits once he has spent down to the applicable amount.

Spending Down

If a person has more assets than Medicaid will allow, she will need to spend them down to the required limits before she can be eligible for benefits. Obviously, one way to accomplish this is for the applicant to pay for the cost of care until she no longer has the funds to do so, or she has spent down to the CSRA. However, many people would like to accelerate the spend-down process so that they can become eligible more quickly, and possibly retain some assets for their families. Although Medicaid seeks to limit the transfer of assets, there are some strategies to accomplish this.

First, a person can spend money to convert a countable asset (cash) to a non-countable asset, such as his home or car. He can pay off his mortgage, make repairs, such as a new roof or air conditioning unit, and improvements, such as making the home more accessible. She can buy a new car or van, which can be used by family members to transport her. She can pay for eyeglasses, dental work, and personal care items, such as incontinence supplies and skincare products, that she will be using once she is on Medicaid.

Medicaid will require documentation, such as canceled checks, to confirm that funds were used for the applicant and

2 The minimum CSRA is $23,184. If the couple's countable assets are worth less than $46,368, the Community Spouse can retain this minimum amount, even if it is more than half of the couple's total countable assets.

his household to spend down to the required level. A penalty will be assessed if the person has transferred assets (other than to his spouse) without receiving value in return within the five years prior to applying for Medicaid, for the purpose of becoming eligible for benefits. Although it is technically possible for someone to demonstrate that he had no way of knowing that he would be applying for benefits when he made gifts to his children (for example, if he is relatively young, and his claim for benefits follows a sudden incident, rather than a progressive condition), most states make the burden of proving this extremely high. For example, even if a "transfer" was the result of exploitation, and was not voluntary at all, many states will require the person to make criminal charges against the person who has taken his money to overcome the presumption that the transfer was for the purpose of qualifying for benefits.

Some people mistakenly believe that if a person's assets are held by a trust, the assets will not be counted by Medicaid. However, assets held by a revocable trust are counted, because the person retains control of those assets. Assets held by an irrevocable trust may not be counted, but transferring assets to the irrevocable trust is governed by the same rules as transfers to another person.

You will notice that a penalty is assessed if the person transferred assets without receiving value in return. If the applicant can demonstrate that he did receive value in return, then the transaction is not a disqualifying transfer. For example, if the applicant's daughter provides care services, such as housecleaning, meal preparation and transportation, for which the applicant would otherwise have to pay a non-related service provider, he can pay his daughter, as long as they enter into a written agreement, and the daughter keeps track of the time spent or services provided as described in that agreement. If the applicant has moved in with a family member, she can purchase a "life estate" in their home, as long as the price reflects the purchaser's actuarial lifespan, as contained in tables incorporated into the Medicaid regulations. Finally, there are certain "humanitarian" exceptions to the assessment of a penalty for transfers within five years of applying. These include transfers to a special needs trust for a disabled child of the applicant, or the transfer of the applicant's home to a child who has been living with the parents and taking care of them for at least two years before the transfer.

This doesn't necessarily mean that a person who may have to apply for Medicaid in the future should never transfer assets to family members. If a senior is relatively healthy, such that it is unlikely that she will need to apply for Medicaid in the next five years, and she feels confident that she can trust her child to set the funds aside in case they should be needed for the parent's care, the gift can always be returned if the parent does need to apply for benefits during that five-year window. In addition, paying the penalty may be a better deal than actually spending down the funds on one's own care. The way the penalty works is that Medicaid calculates the amount of time that an applicant could have paid for care at the "private pay rate," if he had not made the transfer. The private pay rate is an average of the cost of care in a geographic area, but it may not be the actual amount that a person would pay. For example, the current private pay rate in a major metropolitan area other than New York or Los Angeles is $6,646 per month. If an applicant had transferred $20,000, Medicaid would calculate that this would have covered three months' worth of care at the private pay rate, so Medicaid would not pay for the person's care for the first three months after they are otherwise found to be eligible. However, if the actual cost of care is only $3,000 per month, family members who received the transfer could cover the cost of their parents' care for the duration of the penalty period, and still have $11,000 left over.

While Medicaid will cover the full cost of a person's care

in an assisted living or skilled nursing facility, as well as the medical expenses that are not covered by Medicare or other insurance, this coverage may not be free. The Omnibus Budget Reconciliation Act of 1993 ("OBRA") authorized all states to implement an Estate Recovery Program, in order to recoup funds expended on an individual's care during his or her lifetime. This law authorizes states to file a claim against any assets in the estate of a person who received care after the age of 55, that was paid for by its Medicaid program, whether in a facility or at home. This can be accomplished by placing a lien against real property (including both the personal residence and income-producing property that is not counted for purposes of eligibility), or filing a claim against the estate of a person for whom Medicaid had been providing care. In addition, if a person had established an income only trust, or had one of the annuities described above, this law requires that the state Medicaid agency be the primary beneficiary of any funds remaining in those accounts, to the extent necessary to recoup what they had paid.

The Medicaid agency cannot require repayment from an annuity owned by the spouse of the person who had been receiving care, and they cannot place a lien or otherwise seek recovery from property owned by a trust, or owned by the recipient's spouse while the recipient was alive. This is why many Medicaid planners recommend that title to all property that a couple is allowed to retain in the CSRA be transferred to the name of the spouse who is not receiving care. However, even if a couple misses this step, OBRA prohibits the state from seeking recovery from property that was inherited by a spouse, either due to right of survivorship or through a Will. They are also prohibited from seeking recovery from property that is transferred to a disabled spouse or child under the age of 21; property that is the only residence of an heir who lived there for at least a year before the recipient's death; or if the heir operates a business in the property that has been in existence for at least a year and provides at least half of that heir's livelihood.

In addition to the recovery methods authorized under OBRA, states may impose a lien against real property owned by the recipient of Medicaid benefits under amendments to Medicaid law made in the Tax Equity and Fiscal Responsibility Act of 1982 ("TEFRA"). As you might expect, the rules for these TEFRA liens are slightly different than estate recovery under OBRA. This lien will be applied only to the home of a recipient of Medicaid benefits who received care in an institutional setting (rather than at home). However, the lien will not be enforced against Medicaid recipients who are members of Native American tribes, or whose property is occupied by a disabled spouse or child under the age of 21, or if it is occupied by the recipient's sibling who has an equity interest in the home and has been living there for at least a year. It will also not be enforced until the recipient and/or his surviving spouse dies, sells or otherwise transfers the property. It will also not be enforced (because it doesn't apply) if the home is not owned by the recipient, but only by the spouse who did not receive Medicaid services. Finally, the lien is only for the amount actually expended by the Medicaid agency for the recipient's institutional and medical care. All amounts received in excess of that amount are paid to the Medicaid recipient's heirs according to his Will, or the laws of intestate succession.

VA Benefits

Another benefit available to many seniors to help offset the cost of long-term care is the VA Improved Pension with Aid and Attendance Supplement. This needs-based benefit is available to veterans and their surviving spouses who served during wartime (regardless of whether they saw combat or even left the United States), and were not dishonorably discharged. The claimant must document that, due to a medical condition, he requires the "regular aid and attendance" of another, and that his Income for VA Purposes

("IVAP") is less than the maximum benefit amount (in 2013, this is $1,732/month for a single veteran; $2,054/month for a married veteran, and $1,113/month for a surviving spouse). IVAP is calculated by combining the income of both spouses (if applicable) and subtracting the cost of unreimbursed medical expenses. If those expenses include a residential care facility for one or both spouses, IVAP can easily become a negative number, so the claimant would be entitled to the maximum benefit amount. If the expenses are not that great, the VA benefit will make up the difference between the IVAP and the monthly maximum benefit amount.

The VA also applies an asset test to determine whether a claimant is eligible for these benefits. Although the rules are not as clearly defined as they are for Medicaid, practitioners in this field report that the VA will grant benefits to a single claimant whose assets are worth no more than $40,000, and a married claimant with assets worth no more than $80,000. Like Medicaid, the primary residence, vehicle and personal and household goods are not counted. However, unlike Medicaid, income-producing property and certain annuities that might not be counted by state Medicaid agencies are counted by the VA. It is, therefore, critical to consider both the benefits and the criteria for both Medicaid and VA benefits before re-structuring one's assets to apply for one of these programs, as you would not want to inadvertently exclude yourself from eligibility for the other program unless you specifically decided to do so.

One reason why someone might choose to apply for VA benefits, rather than Medicaid, is because currently there is no "look back period" or transfer penalty. Technically, a person could transfer assets to his children during one month, and then apply for benefits, honestly documenting that the value of his assets is less than the maximums described above, the very next month. You should be aware, however, that a couple of bills were introduced in the last session of Congress which would impose a look back period for eligibility for VA benefits. In view of the current focus on reducing costs, it is probably only a matter of time before this idea becomes law.

Choosing the Best Benefit

While it appears that it is easier for a Veteran to qualify for VA benefits than for Medicaid, VA Aid and Attendance has a maximum benefit amount, whereas Medicaid will cover the full cost of the recipient's care (less his share of cost), no matter how much it might be. Also, the CSRA under Medicaid, may allow the spouse to retain more assets than the VA would. On the other hand, the VA benefit is a cash benefit, which can be used to pay for the cost of care in any facility, regardless of whether it is contracted with the state's Medicaid agency, and can cover the cost of more care at home than it may be possible to get the Medicaid agency to provide. The support of an elder law attorney, whose practice is focused on providing the best advice to the senior, based on his or her unique needs and circumstances, (as opposed to a specialist in VA benefits or Medicaid benefits) can be critical in navigating the confusing issues related to choice of benefits.

A Note About Spending Down and Gifting

Several times in the above discussion about qualifying for benefits, we referenced the possibility of making gifts to family members. These decisions should not be made without also consulting with an estate planning attorney (who may or may not be the same person as the elder law attorney) and tax advisor. The same is true about spending down assets in order to qualify for benefits, whether by withdrawing funds from an IRA or paying off a mortgage. Based on your particular circumstances, you might find that the tax consequences of undertaking these actions in order to qualify for benefits to pay for long-term care will cost as much or more as the amount of the benefits for which you are hoping to qualify. In that case, you may want to pull together all of these advisors, including your elder law attorney, to decide what strategy makes the best sense for you and your family, and over what time frame it should be implemented.

32 PUTTING IT ALL TOGETHER: INVESTMENTS, ADVISORS AND YOUR LEGACY TEAM

In our lives, much of what we think about is the future: as children, we think about adulthood; as students, we think about more education and careers evolving from that education. Personally, there are thoughts of marriage and children. Once we are in the workforce, we consider acquisitions, upward mobility, and a successful livelihood. With children, we want to help them launch their good lives with appropriate education. And, everyone at some point has thoughts of retirement.

All of this thinking should also involve planning, which should not be done alone or done without critical information and necessary skills. A core piece of advice regardless of which life stage you are at is to immediately start pulling together your team. Thats the people you trust to give you useful and timely advice. You also should prepare yourself to understand and utilize the advice they are given.

You probably already have sort of a team. Pondering a question, whom do you consult first? For many people, the answer is their spouse, although those extended discussions might be discounted as just conversation. But consider the really trustworthy advice you get from a loved one. It may not be your only source of advice, but, under most circumstances, that may be the only person you can trust completely. The same may be said of conversations with an adult child, a parent or a sibling. Whoever that go to person is in your life, you already have a readily accessible team member. So, don't ignore them.

Nonetheless, a wise person looks beyond the immediate horizon. You are surrounded by a veritable bevy of team members. Consider them and what they can offer you. Much of this book has been geared to discussing those decisions you can make that will allow your assets to flourish and be preserved for retirement and for your beneficiaries. Your estate planning specialists specifically focus on the long term view of your estate. Keep in mind that planning is not simply a grand document prepared in detail to solve all your problems and be put on a shelf. It is a rather constant process. Throughout this book, we have described methods of protecting your assets, reducing your taxes, shielding yourself from liabilities, fostering financial growth and preserving enough of your estate to live on in later life. In the ordinary course of the lifetime of a successful person or couple, there is no one point in time that defines the proper plan for an entire life. A good relationship with your team of experts will both keep you educated about the latest rules and help you make periodic tax and estate plan adjustments that will ensure your goals are met. Like a medical check up, it doesn't have to be expensive to be necessary. Here are some examples of team members you should have in place.

Your personal attorney or your business attorney should not be the person you consult only in an emergency, but instead someone you consult regularly about significant decisions you need to make or about the ongoing operations of your business. Sure, you are fully capable of handling most decisions without constant contact with your attorney. But if you and your business are thriving, it would be a mistake to assume there are no legal implications of your work. Yet, how long has it been since you visited with your business attorney? Or, if you are not in business, how long has it been since you consulted your personal attorney? Consider your attorney to be a good resource and, for most questions, a very good starting point.

The same advice holds for your tax attorney. Whether you are an employee saving your money, investing and accumulating assets for retirement or a business owner with employees and a board of directors or an independent contractor working for multiple U.S. and foreign companies, you have tax issues. Many people find this out after the fact when they see how their simple estate turns into 20 pages of tax forms to be filed at the end of a year. And possibly some prior year amended returns needing to be filed as well. Many people are quite capable of handling basic tax matters themselves, often with the aid of a good accountant (and, ideally, a good bookkeeper as well). But, you don't know, what you don't know. A regular tax check-up with your tax attorney, or at least with your CPA (preferably, sometime between April and December) can help you head off expensive mistakes and lost opportunities. A few minutes reading or watching the business news should convince you that the tax code is in a perpetual state of flux and that it is helpful, and even necessary, to have regular advice from someone paying attention to the latest tax details. It is challenging keeping tabs on new laws and new rules.

Most of us seem to suffer from the "I can handle it myself" syndrome. Few businesses have mentors, and yet most small businesses fail or struggle unnecessarily. Along the way, you have probably worked with someone who taught you a lot about your business or you have probably spent time with business people whose wisdom helped nudge you toward success. If you've ever gotten good advice, imagine getting that good advice on a regular basis. Your business consultants can give you regular helpful input. So, don't ignore them. Make them part of your team. (By the way, you yourself have a great deal of expertise. Imagine sharing that expertise with someone anxious to succeed, anxious to make you one of their advisors. It just makes sense.)

A financial advisor is critical to have in place. Not only do markets change daily, but each of us needs a long term plan. We also need a short and medium term plan. We need someone to ask for quick advice on major expenditures (*e.g.,* should I buy or lease my next car?) as well as long-term planning. Unless we are willing to devote 100% of our time and effort over the next several years becoming fully educated and keeping up with change about financial markets and investment strategies, it makes sense to use the advice and services of someone who does that work for a living.

Your banker is also someone with whom you probably have regular dealings. Have you ever attended one of their free sessions or set up an appointment with one of their business advisory group teams? Your bank or other investors make money when you make money, so they are often a great place to look for support and critical advice, particularly about the bottom line. And, of course, your financiers are your major source for acquiring and keeping good credit.

Your insurance representative is another important member of your legacy team. Remember that good agents do more than sell life insurance. Most agents offer regular insurance audits to review your situation and make insurance and related recommendations for you to consider in the short term and long term.

You need to make sure you put the whole package together: your active short-term income investments, long-term legacy investments, estate plan documents, insurance choices, business organization, personal and business tax advice, banking options, etc. The advice you get from every team member should be coordinated with the advice you get from every other team member. This may sound overly complicated. But it is probably what most of us already do without much deliberation. Go one step further and actively introduce your advisors to each other and convene an advisory meeting. Think of your advisors as your Legacy Team.

In perusing your field of options, don't forget to include the full range of benefits and programs offered by your employer. Often, employers have designated counselors ready to assist you concerning the options offered and trained to evaluate how each option might fit into your financial plan. Some employers offer regular information sessions so you can learn more about these programs.

Government, too, offers lots of information and services and lots of free advice. If you plan to receive Social Security benefits, for example, there is a bounty of information available, there are non-profit organizations offering training and advice, and, of course, there are Social Security representatives who are supposed to assist you and answer your questions.

Implicit in each of these categories is the need for information. You cant buy happiness, but much of what has been discussed in this book has been about the money it takes to get you the freedom you need to attain whatever you personally define as happiness. It is said that even the lowest wage earners the ones who need money the most fail to take the deductions and credits they are legally entitled to on their income tax filings. A little bit of knowledge about taxes would yield them money in the pocket and, thus, more of what life has to offer them. The moral is that, at every level of income, knowledge about money is essential. If you are in business, you know this lesson very well already. But you need to give no less attention to the money that flows into your personal pocket. Learning the rules about money and investing and finance and taxes is part of planning a profitable life.

Many people seek out advice after the fact, which is, in many ways, counterintuitive. In other words, if you want advice on how to get somewhere, you would logically seek that advice before you step one foot in front of the other. But thats not human nature. One can be quite successful and know nothing about high finance. Many, many financially successful people with children have no estate plan and no life insurance. But the safer approach is to be a bit more methodical. One need not be rigid. Just develop a reasonable plan that can be tweaked now and then as needed. For example, think about what would constitute a successful life and what it ordinarily takes to get there. Certainly intelligence, working skills, good health and other assets are needed. There are lots of formulas for financial success. For example, if you manage to put $25,000 in the bank every year (and never touch it), you will have over $1 million at retirement and that can yield $50,000-100,000 of income per year to live on. Another example is by putting $7,000 in the bank every year will later put one or two children comfortably through college. The moral is that you need to think about what constitutes success and then specifically find out, by research and by consulting your Legacy Team, how to get there.

Making long term investments to support your eventual retirement and to put children through college are only two of the many major financial decisions you will face in your life. You will also buy a house or maybe several houses in succession, of ever increasing value and ever increasing mortgage levels. Having children in the first place is a major financial decision. Returning to school to re-tool would be a significant economic decision. Supporting aging parents might be on your eventual horizon as well. And, of course, there are major financial catastrophes that you have to plan for, while hoping they will never occur. With the advice of your Legacy Team members, and armed with up-to-date information and the types of planning tools presented in this book, you should develop a flexible portfolio that gives structure to your efforts to achieve a successful and financially secure life.

As a final word, does this seem like a crowded and expensive gaggle of advisors? It really is not. For example, you take your car in for regular check ups or regular oil changes or when the manufacturer recommends a consultation. You also take your car in when there's a problem. Often, your car expert will tell you that your car has a problem festering and that needs watching. Then the problem is not a surprise and other parts of the car have not been damaged by the breakdown of one item. Using your Legacy Team in the same way can help you ward off future problems. It is so much easier to put in plans and safeguards than to fix something that has already gone wrong. Don't go it alone!

33 GLOSSARY

The terms used in this book are legal terms which are generally utilized nationally to address estate, asset protection, and tax issues. This glossary is not meant to be all inclusive, but it is designed to help the reader in deciphering the meaning of the words used in the discussions and hopefully makes these materials even more user-friendly. To the extent possible, common language will be used in defining terms.

Adult – Legally, an adult is considered to be age 18 or older or otherwise is emancipated.

Annuity – An annuity can be commercial or private and refers to a contract which creates a stream of income payable to a person, for a term of years or life, with the amount of the payment based on an initial contribution of principal and a rate of return for income. The person who is the Annuitant is the measuring life.

Ascertainable Standard – The ascertainable standard means the measure for health, education, maintenance and support ("HEMS") that a trustee may utilize in making principal distributions to a trust beneficiary. While interpretation of the needs of the beneficiary for "HEMS" is fairly discretionary, a HEMS standard will enable a beneficiary and probably her creditors to demand trust principal distributions.

Attorney-in-Fact – The attorney-in-fact is the agent named to act for the principal under a power of attorney.

Basis – Basis in an asset is what was paid for it or what the donor paid for it. Special rules exist for most estate-owned property.

Beneficiary – A person who receives distributions from an estate, from a trust, or from contracts which have beneficiary designations, such as IRAs, pension funds, annuities, and life insurance policies, is a beneficiary.

Charging Order – A charging order is obtained from the court to authorize a judgment creditor to be an assignee of a limited partnership or limited liability company interest owned by the debtor as part of the debtor's satisfaction of the judgment.

Charity – A charity is an organization which has been designated as a tax-exempt entity under the terms of IRC Sec. 501(c)(3) and related sections. As such, the charity can be a public charity which receives the bulk of its funding from the general public; a private foundation which is supported by charitable gifting of a few people; and a church and a school, which are recognized by the Internal Revenue Service as valid religious or educational entities.

Code – Code refers in this writing to the Internal Revenue Code of 1986, as amended.

Codicil – A codicil is a written amendment to a Will.

Commissioner of Internal Revenue – Sometimes abbreviated as "CIR" or "Comm'r." the Commissioner is head of the Internal Revenue Service.

Consanguinity – Consanguinity means that persons are descended from the same ancestor. They are related "by blood" or are of the same bloodline.

Conservatorship – The term refers to the court proceeding and the resultant estate created when a person is appointed to manage the assets of a minor or other person who is incapable of managing his financial affairs. Some states use the word guardianship for this purpose.

Consideration – Consideration is one of the elements of a contract and refers to the thing of value given in exchange for a service or a transfer of property. Consideration is the purchase price paid for a house, groceries, gasoline, a hair cut, or for performance under a contract.

Corporation – A corporation is created under state laws. To validly do business, it must be registered and follow certain formalities. Generally, a corporation must have in its title one of the following words: Corporation, Company, Incorporated, Limited or abbreviations of those words such as Corp., Co., Inc., or Ltd.

Credit Shelter Trust – A credit shelter trust, also known as a bypass trust or "B" trust (in an A-B trust combination) is the trust set up to receive the lesser of the deceased spouse's assets or his estate tax exemption amount, so that those assets are not included in the estate of the surviving spouse for estate tax purposes. The term "credit" is used because the estate tax exemption is technically expressed as a tax credit.

Decedent – The decedent is a deceased individual, in legal terms.

Disclaim – To disclaim a gift or an inheritance is to refuse to accept it. In a disclaimer, the gift or inheritance will pass to the next person in the blood line of the disclaiming donee or to a credit shelter trust for a surviving spouse.

Donee – The donee means the person who has received a gift.

Donor – The donor is the person who makes a gift of her own assets.

Emancipation – A minor is considered emancipated or free from the disability of minority under state law if she is married or otherwise declared to be emancipated by a court regardless of being under age 18.

Estate – The term refers to the assets owned by a person at his death (his "estate"), the assets owned by a trust (the "trust estate"), and the assets managed in a conservatorship (the "conservatorship estate").

Estate Tax – Estate tax means a federal tax on the value of one's estate at death. The tax is calculated on the net fair market value of the property in the estate and is all-inclusive of real property, personal effects and other personal property, money, life insurance owned by the decedent, pension funds, and property subject to a power of appointment if the decedent can appoint it to herself. Some states have separate estate taxes as well.

Executor – The person named in a will to administer the decedent's estate is called the executor or in many states, the personal representative.

Fiduciary – A fiduciary is a person who has undertaken to perform special acts for the benefit of another person. It is a relationship of trust, involving the highest degree of duty. Trustees, personal representatives or executors, guardians, conservators, attorneys-in-fact, health care agents, employers with respect to employee withholding taxes are all examples of fiduciaries.

Generation-Skipping – Generation-skipping refers to an estate planning practice of skipping generations in the distribution of wealth. A parent might skip her children's generation and leave everything in the estate to the grandchildren. The concept was developed as a tax-savings device by wealthy families, and is now subject to a special tax, a generous exemption, and complex tax rules.

Gift – A gift is something of value which is transferred by the owner to another person without consideration or promise required, with all ownership and control being transferred to the recipient, the donee. A gift which is revocable or short-term may not be a completed gift.

Gift Tax – The gift tax is a federal transfer tax placed on the transferor and determined by the value of the net gift made. States generally do not impose gift taxes. The gift tax owed is reduced by the annual exclusion and a person's gift tax exemption.

Guardian Ad Litem – A guardian ad litem is a court-appointed adult to represent the interests of children or incapacitated persons. Often, a guardian ad litem is used in actions for divorce, child abuse, and contested probates.

Guardianship – The term refers to a court proceeding and the resulting relationship in which a person is appointed to make decisions for a person who is a minor or who lacks the mental capacity to make health care and daily living decisions for himself. A parent is the natural guardian of her minor child. Some states also use the term synonymously with <u>conservatorship</u>.

Heir – An heir is a person entitled by law to an inheritance from an estate, but not all heirs actually receive anything as a beneficiary.

HEMS – *See* Ascertainable Standard. It stands for "health, education, maintenance and support."

Incapacity – There are two kinds of incapacity: a minor is incapacitated because the minor has no independent rights under the law, including the ability to own property; and an adult is incapacitated if he lacks the mental ability to handle his financial affairs or make medical and other decisions for himself. ("adult incapacity"). Adult incapacity is usually determined by a court in a finding of incompetency.

Income – For tax and related purposes, income is generally considered to be earnings of interest, dividends, rents, and royalties, as well as earned income such as salary, wages, and other payments for services.

Inheritance Tax – An inheritance tax is levied on the recipient of an inheritance, which are assets received from an estate. The tax is calculated on the value of what is received. It is usually a tax levied by various states, although the number of states using an inheritance tax is shrinking as many states have adopted their own versions of an estate tax.

Inter Vivos – This term from Latin means "during life." An inter vivos trust is made during the trustor's lifetime.

Internal Revenue Service – As part of the Department of Treasury, the Internal Revenue Service ("IRS") is charged with the enforcement of tax laws and collection of taxes at the federal level.

IRA – The term is short for individual retirement account, which is governed by Code Section 408. It is a personal tax-free account set up by an individual, which must be managed by a qualifying financial institution as custodian of the funds.

Issue – Issue refers to a person's children and all direct descendants thereafter. A father's issue would include his children, grandchildren, great grandchildren, and on down the line.

LLC – This term is short for limited liability company, a type of entity created under state laws, usually for business purposes. While all 50 states have LLCs, the statutes describing and governing LLCs vary, sometimes widely from state to state.

Majority – Age eighteen (18) is the age of majority.

Marital Trust – A marital trust is usually a subtrust set up in a Will or revocable living trust to hold the share available for the surviving spouse. Properly structured, it will not be the subject to estate taxes at the death of the first spouse.

Minority – Persons under age eighteen (18) who have not otherwise been emancipated are minors. Minority is considered a legal disability, requiring guardianship, usually by parents, and conservatorship, if the minor holds any assets in his own name.

Net Value – As used herein, net value refers to the fair market value of an asset, whether it is real or personal property, less any liabilities which encumber it. Liabilities can include a mortgage, judgment lien, or other form of levy.

Operation of Law – This is a property transfer term which means that title (ownership) to real or personal property passes to another person by statutory or common law. It is often used to describe how a surviving joint tenants receives sole ownership of property ("by operation of law") at the death of the co-owner when the titling is "joint tenancy with right of survivorship."

Partnership – Partnership refers to a business relationship between two or more parties in which they agree on a common goal or activity, expecting to receive and share profits and losses. It is a form of legal entity, and has specific tax rules under the Code at Subchapter K. In a general partnership, which can be formed without official filings, each partner can bind the entity in contract, and each is jointly and severally responsible for its debts. In a limited partnership, only the general partner can bind the entity and is personally responsible for its debts.

Personal Property – Personal property is all property which is not real estate. Examples include stocks and bonds, jewelry, cars, furnishing, clothing, equipment, livestock, etc.

Power of Appointment – A power of appointment is the authority given a person through a Will, trust or other instrument, entitling and enabling the recipient of the power to name herself or a third party as the beneficiary of the object of the power. There can be tax consequences to the recipient if she can name herself or if she lets the power lapse without naming a third party.

Principal – For trust purposes, generally the principal is the group of assets owned by the trust as distinguished from the income earned by those assets. For example, stock would be the principal, and the income would be the dividends paid to the owner of the stock. Principal also refers to the person who sets up a power of attorney and benefits from its use.

Probate – For estate purposes, probate is a process which takes place in state or local court to grant a person legal authority to handle a deceased person's estate. Probate proceedings are also used to determine the authenticity of a Will, resolve creditor issues of the deceased, and adjudicate rights of beneficiaries.

Property – This term, standing alone, refers to any asset, whether it is real estate or personal property. In essence, it means all "things" or assets which can be owned, tangible and intangible.

Qualified Domestic Trust or "QDOT" – A QDOT is a special trust, required for the marital deduction against estate taxes, when the surviving spouse is not a U.S. citizen. It must have a U.S. trustee, and principal distributions to the surviving spouse are subject immediately to U.S. estate taxes.

Qualified Terminable Interest Property Trust or "QTIP" Trust – A QTIP trust is a specialized trust with special rules designed to hold the deceased spouse's assets for the surviving spouse, with disposition of the assets provided by the deceased spouse in his estate planning documents and qualifying for the 100% marital deduction against the deceased spouse's estate for estate taxes. A QTIP trust can also be set up as recipient of a lifetime gift.

Real Property – Real property refers to all forms of real estate: land, any and all improvements on land, and properly created condominium air space.

Regs. – This abbreviation is short for Treasury Regulations, which explain and complement the provisions of the Internal Revenue Code.

Self-Settled Trust – This term refers to a trust which a person has set up for his own benefit, such as a revocable living trust which first benefits the settlor (or trustor) during his lifetime.

Settlor – Settlor describes the person who creates a trust. It is often used interchangeably with the term <u>trustor</u> or <u>grantor</u>.

Spendthrift – Spendthrift describes a person who spends wastefully. Spendthrift provisions in trusts, and often as set forth in state trust laws, protect trust assets from the creditors of a trust beneficiary.

Trust – A trust is an entity formed by a three-part relationship among 1) the trustor who creates the trust; 2) the trustee who holds and manages the property interest in the trust estate; and 3) the beneficiary or beneficiaries who receive economic or other benefits from the trust assets or trust estate.

Trustee – The term refers to the person or entity serving as the fiduciary of a trust. The trustee is empowered by law and by the trust agreement to manage, keep and invest the trust estate and to make distributions to the beneficiaries.

Trustor – This word describes the person who creates a trust. It is often used in place of the term <u>settlor</u> or <u>grantor</u>.

Uniform Transfers to Minors Act – Also referred to by the initials "UTMA," the Uniform Transfers to Minors Act provides a custodian procedure for an adult to be the custodian over gifts made to a minor. A minor by legal definition is prohibited from owning assets on his own until he reaches majority age. UTMA is adopted by the various states, and the rules are part of state statutes. Some states continue to use the older terminology of Uniform Gifts to Minors Act or "UGMA," in which the rules are slightly different.

SNEAK PEEK

More great ideas are coming in the sequel to *Your Life ... Your Legacy, a Legal Handbook*, with planned publication in 2015. Additional tools for advanced tax, estate, and business planning will be offered. Those readers with more complicated asset holdings, business or investment interests, and asset protection needs will find leading-edge concepts and resources. Or, if you are just a hearty reader interested in self-improvement, go for it!

Adding to the veritable alphabet soup of planning tools presented here in *Your Life*, topics in the sequel will include SCINs, private offerings, charitable trusts, captive insurance, GRATs, IDGTs, LLC flips, trust decanting, and BDITs, to name a few.

Email us at askdarra@gmail.com to reserve your copy.